EXETER

Remembering 1914–18

AF212067

DAVID PARKER
IN ASSOCIATION WITH THE
DEVON AND EXETER INSTITUTION

The History Press

To my son Neil and daughter Cheryl
— with love

First published 2014

The History Press
The Mill, Brimscombe Port
Stroud, Gloucestershire, GL5 2QG
www.thehistorypress.co.uk

British Library Cataloguing in Publication Data.
A catalogue record for this book is available from the British Library.

ISBN 978 0 7509 6026 7

Typesetting and origination by The History Press
Printed in Great Britain

CONTENTS

Timeline

1914

28 June
Assassination of Archduke Franz Ferdinand in Sarajevo

3 August
Conservative garden party hosted by Henry Duke, the city's MP

4 August
Great Britain declares war on Germany

10 August
Mayoress of Exeter's War Relief Depot established

22 August
434 Exeter men enlisted to date

23 August
Battle of Tannenberg commences

6 September
First Battle of the Marne

25 September
Exeter Committee for the Relief of War Refugees established

4 October
West of England Eye Infirmary becomes Exeter's Number 1 War Emergency Hospital, and opens three days later

19 October
First Battle of Ypres

1915

25 April
Allied landing at Gallipoli

7 May
Germans torpedo and sink the Lusitania

31 May
First German Zeppelin raid on London

9 September
King George V and Queen Mary visit Exeter's war emergency hospitals

20 December
Allies finish their evacuation of and withdrawal from Gallipoli

1916

24 January

The British Government introduces conscription

21 February

Battle of Verdun commences

31 May

Battle of Jutland

4 June

Brusilov Offensive commences

30 June

Thomas Bailey of Exeter imprisoned as a conscientious objector

1 July

First day of the Battle of the Somme with 57,000 British casualties

Devonshire Regiment battalions engage in the attack on Pozières

27 August

Italy declares war on Germany

18 December

Battle of Verdun ends

6 April

The United States declares war on Germany

1917

31 July

Third Battle of Ypres (Passchendaele)

9 April

Battle of Arras

20 August

Third Battle of Verdun

17 October

Heavitree Parochial Boys' School horse chestnut collection reaches 3 cwt

26 October

Second Battle of Passchendaele

20 November

Battle of Cambrai

7 December

USA declares war on Austria-Hungary

1918

3 March
Russia and the Central Powers sign the Treaty of Brest-Litovsk

21 March
Second Battle of the Somme

27 May
2nd Battalion Devonshire Regiment holds Bois de Butte in the Third Battle of the Aisne

15 July
Second Battle of the Marne

8 August
Battle of Amiens, first stage of the Hundred Days Offensive

22 September
The Great Allied Balkan victory

27 September
Storming of the Hindenburg Line

18 October
Dorothy Prouse, city tram conductor, dies of influenza, aged 24

8 November
Armistice negotiations commence

9–10 November
Kaiser Wilhelm II abdicates, Germany is declared a republic

11 November
Armistice Day, cessation of hostilities on the Western Front

1919

19 July
Exeter's Peace Day procession in pouring rain

ACKNOWLEDGEMENTS

This book is based largely upon a host of primary sources. They include the letters, diaries, memoirs, magazines, newspapers, school logbooks, city council minutes and reports, and files from various wartime committees and organisations deposited in the Devon and Exeter Institution in the Cathedral Close and the Devon Heritage Centre in Sowton.

I am grateful to the staff of the Heritage Centre and colleagues at the Devon and Exeter Institution for their readily given advice and support. My thanks go to Su Conniff, Sadru Bhanji and Darren Marsh for their help in identifying documents and finding many of the illustrations. I owe much to the critical interest taken in my research by my ex-university colleagues and friends Chris Lee, Bill Leedham and Tony Ovens. The errors that remain are all mine.

In particular, I am pleased to take this opportunity to offer my thanks to Tony Ovens for taking all of the pictures in this book, many of them from poor quality images in contemporary newspapers. It was a time-consuming and skilled task, and I am very grateful.

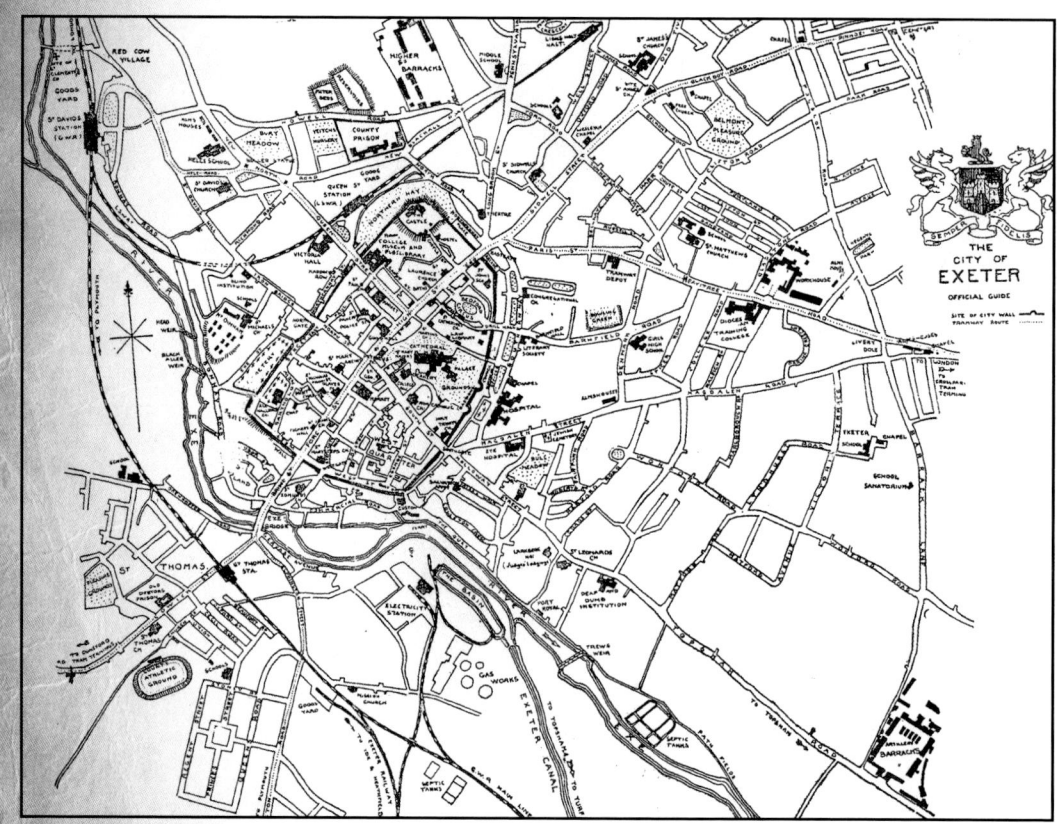

Map of Exeter just before the First World War. (Devon and Exeter Institution)

INTRODUCTION

The murder of Archduke Franz Ferdinand, heir to the Austro-Hungarian throne, merited a brief mention in the *Exeter Flying Post* on 28 June 1914, just as it had in the British national newspapers. Regular readers would have known that assassination was an occupational hazard for Continental royal families at this time. King Umberto I of Italy, Grand Duke Sergei (uncle of Tsar Nicholas II), King Alexander I of Serbia, King Carlos of Portugal and the Empress Elisabeth, the consort of Emperor Franz Joseph of Austria-Hungary, had all died violent deaths within the last quarter of a century.

Franz Ferdinand and his wife had been visiting Sarajevo, the capital of Bosnia, and their shooting by dissident Serbs provided a ready excuse for Austria-Hungary to chastise Serbia for opposing its annexation of neighbouring Bosnia and Herzegovina in 1908. It seemed a minor Balkan affair, but a disastrous chain reaction was set in motion. Austria-Hungary presented Serbia with a humiliating ultimatum that would reduce it to almost a satellite state, and declared war the moment it was rejected on 28 July. Russia, Serbia's Slav ally, then started to mobilise its armies against Austria-Hungary, its long-standing Balkan rival. On 30 July, Germany mobilised in support of its ally, Austria-Hungary, and demanded that France, Russia's ally, stayed neutral. France said nothing, but its armies were mobilised by 2 August when German troops invaded Belgium and approached the French border. On 4 August, Great Britain declared war on Germany when it ignored its ultimatum to withdraw from Belgium.

The war was far from being all about Serbia. In 1904, Great Britain had signed the *Entente Cordiale* with France that fell short of a military alliance but nevertheless publicly signalled its deep suspicions of Germany's rising naval might, commercial rivalry and aggressive empire building. Not surprisingly, this did nothing to stem Imperial Germany's ambitions. And an almost forgotten treaty of 1839 ensured that Great Britain, which was always wary of hostile powers establishing control over the major Channel ports opposite its shores, would preserve the de facto independence of Belgium.

In practice, Germany's declaration of war on Russia meant that its armies had to defeat France first – and quickly – before Russia's vast forces had time to mount a serious attack from the east. In order to achieve this, Germany planned a massive curved attack through north-east France aimed directly at Paris, and Belgium lay right in the path of the intended invasion route. In the event, the plan failed – just. German forces were brought to a halt, and within a few weeks Germany faced the war on two fronts it had feared. Ironically, in 1890 it was Germany that had thrown France and Russia together when the impetuous new kaiser, Wilhelm II, refused to renew a treaty of mutual support with Russia because it opposed Germany's growing influence in the Balkans.

Lying on the River Exe a few miles from the South Devon coast, the ancient city of Exeter seemed a long way from the battlefields as the interminable conflict seized nation after nation in its grip and rapidly spread across the globe. Yet local families and institutions were caught up in the war from its outset. City men served in many different regiments and warships, and participated in numerous battles on land and sea. Over 900 were killed, and many more injured. Exeter was always full of men in uniform – in training, in transit, on leave, or recovering from wounds or illnesses. The city's women endured the agonising silences between news from their menfolk and, worst of all, the fear of a knock on the door with a telegram boy's news of the death of a loved one. They coped with busy family lives as best they could, but hundreds of women from all social classes helped to raise thousands of pounds for wartime charities, readily took over the absent men's jobs, and ensured the city's war emergency hospitals wanted for nothing in their care of thousands of casualties.

Despite the censorship, the city was never short of wartime news. Although the build up to military initiatives was kept secret, once they were underway news of their progress – initially celebratory, but invariably more measured soon afterwards – quickly reached the city through newspapers, letters home and men on leave or in hospital. The horrors of war became public knowledge long before the end of 1914 – the earth-pounding and ear-shattering noise of bombardments, the sudden deaths of comrades standing nearby, the bodies blown to bits, the shattered trenches, cloying mud, ever-present rats and lice, and the terrifying advances on enemy positions. The descriptions of battles and the long lists of casualties kept appearing, and the dreadful attrition rate helped power not only the endless recruitment drives, but also the controversies over why so many men failed to enlist, or sought exemption when conscription was introduced in 1916.

In sharp contrast to the generally dark wartime news, more ordinary things went on in the city. There were films, plays and revues to enjoy – and not all of them were connected with the war. The very popular bicycling and motorcycling clubs remained active, the city's cafés and restaurants did well, and days out to the seaside and the moors resumed their familiar role as moments to escape from the world of work – and family worries. Although some European imports were badly affected, most shops adjusted quickly and remained well stocked, at least until the weeks of food shortages in 1917 and 1918. Clothing and furniture and other household goods remained readily available, and at all prices. There was a semblance of normality, but that was all it was.

The newspapers are now brittle, the letters fragile, and the bindings of diaries and memoirs are falling apart. But the contents of these fading documents still shine a bright light on the aspirations and anxieties of local people during more than four years of unprecedented conflict. When the fighting finally ground to a halt, nothing would ever be quite the same as it had been before.

This book is about what it was like to be in the City of Exeter during these momentous years, during which every human emotion must have been stretched to breaking point – and sometimes beyond.

1

OUTBREAK OF WAR

For much of 1914, domestic issues dominated local newspapers in Exeter, much like elsewhere in the country. The violent tactics of militant suffragettes – setting fire to pillar boxes, damaging works of art, disturbing religious services, burning churches, and smashing shop windows – incited sonorous editorial condemnation in the *Flying Post*, especially when a Venetian watercolour by the Exeter artist John Shapland was ruined in London's Doré Gallery. A great deal of space was devoted to well-attended meetings of Exeter's branch of the League for Opposing Women's Suffrage. Women speakers delighted their audiences with assertions that only men could enforce laws and therefore only men should make them, that equal pay was nonsense as equal work was impossible, and that working-class women would not know what to do with the vote if they possessed it.

THE PANKHURSTS,
VOTES FOR WOMEN & THE WAR
Mrs Emmeline Pankhurst (1858–1928) founded the Women's Social and Political Union in 1903. Dedicated to female suffrage, it achieved notoriety through its confrontation with an intransigent government through violent attacks on private and public property. Two of Mrs Pankhurst's daughters, Adela and Sylvia, began to oppose the mounting violence, and in 1914 the rift became official when Mrs Pankhurst and third daughter Christabel supported the war, whilst Adela and Sylvia campaigned for peace and against conscription – and even hid conscientious objectors.

However, not everyone in the city was opposed to giving women the vote. In December 1913, Mrs Pankhurst was arrested on the White Start liner RMS *Majestic* at Plymouth and taken to Exeter Prison, where she went on hunger strike. Suffragettes flocked there from across the city, county and country but had to endure insults and 'rough horse-play' from groups of local men. One suffragette was only just saved from falling over the parapet of the nearby railway bridge. In May 1914, Canon Masterman of Exeter Cathedral and Sir Henry Hepburn, Vice-Chairman of Devon County Council, spoke publicly in favour of enfranchising women. It would, they claimed, enrich women's lives and help break down the barriers of party politics.

Another issue working local editors into frenzies was the alleged threats to national stability and prosperity posed by the wave of crippling strikes and what many thought were their driving force, the destructive creed of Socialism. In 1912, Exeter felt the force of a national coal strike and a sympathetic walk-out by many railway workers. Local quarries, paper mills and Messrs Willey's extensive iron foundries on Exe Island were forced to close. City charities reopened their soup kitchens and

Drifting towards domestic disaster. H.H. Asquith, the Prime Minister, is rowing the boat. (Trewman's Flying Post, *13.6.14)*

DRIFTING.

JOHN BULL :— For heaven's sake stop that noise and look where we're going!

clothing centres, and the police helped distribute the dwindling stock of coal to needy families. In the summer of 1914 a bitter, and sometimes violent, strike erupted in the Teign Valley granite quarries a few miles outside Exeter, and on 1 August 1914 building workers within the city downed tools. Labour relations were distinctly poor, and social unrest widespread and deeply worrying.

Alongside the threats posed by the suffragettes, Socialists and strikers, the city newspapers reported that the home rule controversy in Ireland was spiralling out of control. By 1914, both the Irish Nationalists and the Ulster Unionists possessed armed paramilitary forces, enabling the former to rise up in arms against any attempt by the British Government to renege on home rule and the latter to oppose the imposition of Irish Roman Catholic tyranny on Ulster Protestants. Henry Duke, Exeter's Conservative MP, was a fervent Unionist and frequently spoke to appreciative city audiences about the perils facing Irish Protestants, especially in the north. Civil war seemed inevitable as 1914 dawned and the September date set for home rule drew near. In December 1913, a train carrying Sir Edward Carson, the charismatic Ulster Unionist leader, to Plymouth stopped at Exeter St David's station. A crowd, including the workmen rebuilding the station, soon gathered around him and cheered his brief speech declaring that Ulstermen would never be placed 'under the heels of the declared enemies of England'.

During the summer of 1914, the kaiser believed that Great Britain was so absorbed with its domestic problems, notably Ireland, that it would do anything to avoid embroilment in a European war. Conversely Herbert Asquith, the British Prime Minister, later acknowledged that the outbreak of the war defused, at least temporarily, a particularly explosive situation within the British Isles. Indeed, on the last day of July 1914, the touchpaper of Irish Civil War could easily have been lit when a British Army unit was attacked by armed Nationalists who had been caught, it was alleged, smuggling weapons and then stoned by an angry crowd. The soldiers opened fire, killing three and wounding sixty protestors.

Exeter lay deep in the West Country, but its relatively small size and provincial position belied its significance in national affairs. It was a historic city, as symbolised by the remains of a Roman legionary fortress, the substantial ruins of Rougemont Castle, the much repaired city walls and the centuries-old Anglican cathedral. It was the centre of Diocese of Exeter affairs and county as well as city administration. All important committee meetings were held there. The barracks of the the Devonshire Regiment (the 'Devons') and a section of Royal Field Artillery were in Exeter, and the county assizes were held in an eighteenth-century courthouse deep within Rougemont Castle. During the war, the city continued to be the natural centre for numerous county and regional organisations concerned with the creation of emergency hospitals, a host of fundraising charities, the settlement of thousands of overseas refugees, and implementing the draconian regulations for the production, distribution and price of food.

In national and city elections Exeter's voters swung between favouring the Liberals and Conservatives, although overall the Conservatives had the edge. In national elections they had given a large majority to the Conservative Sir Edgar Vincent in 1900; just eighty-five to the Liberal Sir George Kekewich in 1906; a mere twenty-six to the Conservative Henry Duke in January 1910; and just one to Duke in December 1910 – but only after two recounts had favoured his Liberal opponent before a formal investigation declared several Liberal votes invalid. The clergy and businessmen within the city, and the country gentry residing just outside it, dominated Exeter's affairs, and it has to be said that the city's Liberals were far from radical while the Conservatives still possessed a touch of *noblesse oblige*.

The population, including Heavitree, was about 59,000 and growing, but only slowly.

THE DEVONS

Raised by the Duke of Beaufort, the regiment became permanent in 1685. It fought in Ireland (1690), and in many battles against the French in the eighteenth century. It became the 11th Regiment of Foot in 1751, and the Devons in 1881. In the Napoleonic Wars it was in the West Indies and then in Spain, earning its nickname the 'Bloody Eleventh' during the Battle of Salamanca (1812). In Queen Victoria's reign it was on Imperial garrison duty, and fought at Ladysmith and Spion Kop in the Boer War (1899–1902). Its motto is the same as the city's – *semper fidelis* (always faithful).

The greatest area of male employment was building and construction, followed by workers in shops and other small businesses, with railway-related jobs coming in third. Domestic service in private houses, great and small, and in commercial properties such as cafés and hotels was by far the greatest employer of women. Dressmaking, either in workshops or as home commissions, was second.

In 1914, roads of great antiquity connected Exeter to other towns, and as more and more motor cars, lorries and charabancs began to use them the *Flying Post* carried notices of small penny-pinching improvement schemes, usually the traditional repacking of stone surfaces but occasionally the tarmacking of a further section of main road. Far more frequent, though, were the newspaper's warnings to travellers in its 'Motoring Matters' column of local hazards such as sharp corners, steep hills, narrow bridges, hidden junctions and the sudden appearance of farmers' wagons, herds of cattle and flocks of sheep.

The streets within the city itself were gradually changing too. In traditional vein, flocks of sheep were still driven to market within Exeter, but the overcrowding of its narrow streets with an assortment of motorised vans and lorries, horse-drawn wagons and carts, and hand-pulled barrows and stalls was causing citizens and city councillors increasing irritation and concern. In 1914 the annual Cart Horse Parade remained a popular spectacle, but by then the newspapers routinely carried advertisements for motor vehicles, and not horse-drawn ones. The large motorcar saleroom and workshops of Reid and Lee were well established in New North Road, and so were those of Standford and White in Sidwell Street, along with Greenslade's charabanc business in Queen Street. 'Motoring Matters' gave readers regular information on the worth of mechanical innovations, the services of local garages, recommended West Country routes, and the heady but highly fashionable pastime of rallying.

In recent decades a few road-widening schemes had been carried out in the city, resulting in a number of historic but obviously unwanted houses and the ancient but redundant Allhallows church being demolished. In the 1880s, a grand new post office and the popular Eastgate Parade shopping centre had been built on the

42 EXETER. — Ex Bridge. — LL

*A flock of sheep
is driven across
Exe Bridge.
(Dr Sadru Bhanji)*

High Street site of the demolished frontage of the pre-Reformation
St John's Hospital. Also in the High Street, the seventeenth-century,
but much repaired, Half Moon Inn was demolished in 1912 and
replaced by the city's richly adorned Dellar's Café in 1916. In 1895
the decision had been taken to widen North Street by slicing off 8ft
of every ancient property on its west side and then rebuilding the
foreshortened fronts in red brick. They are still there.

Early in 1914, widespread debate surrounded plans to
remodel the city centre by extensive demolition and the creation of impressive new public buildings and municipal offices
in Queen Street, adjoining the radically remodelled station.
Far wider pathways would lead from the High Street to Cathedral
Close, extensive city centre gardens would be planted and
several narrow but important road junctions would be turned
into open 'circuses'. The aim was to enhance the flow of traffic,
create a number of attractive vistas and entice more visitors to
a prosperous-looking city combining an ancient cathedral with a
host of easily accessible modern facilities. Inevitably arguments
grew heated and inevitably the war brought them to a halt.

One city innovation proving immensely popular, though, was
the restructured tram system inaugurated in 1905. Electric tram-
cars replaced the horse-drawn ones and the routes were extended.
Lines now ran from Exeter St David's station along Queen Street
to the High Street and Eastgate, from where one line went to

Livery Dole in Heavitree and another along Sidwell Street to the end of Blackboy Road. From the High Street, another route ran along Fore Street and across Exe Bridge and then diverged along Cowick Street or Alphington Street.

The trams had a fine safety record, despite their frequent overcrowding, but in March 1917 a tram running down Fore Street jumped its tracks as it neared Exe Bridge, crashed onto its side, slid until it hit the parapet, lurched into the middle of the road and ground to a halt. A woman who had belatedly jumped off the tram was crushed to death as it tipped over. There was talk that essential maintenance work had not been carried out due to wartime economies and labour shortages.

Road transport remained arduous, but by 1914 Devon's railway system was almost at its maximum extent and heavily used by goods and passenger trains. Exeter was an important junction and this was to be of immense significance throughout the war. From the major London & South West Railway (LSWR) station in Queen Street, a main line ran to London Waterloo via Yeovil and Salisbury, with local branch lines to Exmouth, Sidmouth, Seaton and Lyme Regis.

The first electric tram. (Dr Sadru Bhanji)

COPYRIGHT]   **Opening of the Exeter Electric Trams, April 4th, 1905.**
(CAR DRIVEN BY THE MAYOR, E. C. PERRY, ESQ.)   W. V. COLE, PRINTER.

At the less convenient St David's station, the main Great Western Railway (GWR) lines ran eastwards to London Paddington via Taunton and Reading, with local lines branching off to Tiverton and north Devon. Westwards from St David's, GWR lines ran to Plymouth and Cornwall via a junction at Newton Abbot where another main line branched off to Torquay and Kingswear. In an unusual configuration, LSWR trains also ran from Queen Street to St David's station, from where one line ran through a dozen villages to north Devon and another curved north and west around Dartmoor to Tavistock and Plymouth.

Station placards and newspaper advertisements regularly announced railway excursions, not only to local seaside resorts but also to Bude, Padstow, Bideford, Barnstaple and Ilfracombe on the north coast, and further afield to Salisbury, Bournemouth, Southampton, London and even Paris. Exeter was well connected.

Within the city, short branch lines and numerous sidings served the wharves and important industrial areas each side of the River Exe and its canal. Small cargo ships frequented the city. In one week in April 1914, for example, the *Flying Post* reported that the *Salvador* brought timber from Sweden, the *Gleaner* potatoes from Dunbar, the *Edgar* and *Anne* limestone from Berryhead, the *Sirdar* limestone from Babbacombe, and the *Genesta* cement from London.

The extensive foundries of Henry Willey in Water Lane and Haven Lane manufactured purifiers, pipes, meters and vast holders for the gas industry, and also huge quantities of metal castings for the construction industry and manufacturers of heating and cooking appliances. Other major industries processed, packaged and distributed timber products, paper and stationery, skins and hides, and wine and beer. Kelly's Directory for 1914 shows the high number of small traders and businesses, some no doubt comprising a single person or family – notably hairdressers, dressmakers, collar makers, tailors, bakers, confectioners, fishmongers, butchers, boot and shoe makers, basket makers, cabinet makers, furniture and china repairers, coal dealers, chimney sweeps, nurserymen and gardeners. There were also several electricians and electrical businesses, and Exeter possessed a large power station

The Exe Basin and adjacent foundries and factories. (Dr Sadru Bhanji)

not far from the riverside gasworks and coal yards; the newspapers carried regular advertisements from the gas and electricity companies tempting householders to 'get connected'. Gas and electric cookers were readily available, but still costly, and often were rented.

For an artisan in the city earning about 35/- a week, beer, vegetables and eggs were cheap and he probably possessed a garden and a few chickens and rabbits. However, other items commonly advertised in early 1914, such as new cotton sheets at 5/11d, blankets at 7/11d, cheaper suits at 30/-, a bottle of 'Old Cellar' Scotch Whisky at 4/-, tooth extractions at 1/- and a set of false teeth at 42/- would severely stretch the family budget, and many High Street goods would have been beyond his reach. In 1913–15, advertisements offered indoor parlourmaids as little as £15–22 a year, and cook-housekeepers about £30, but generally they were given rooms, uniforms and meals.

However, the incidence of abject poverty and pauperism within the city was low, and did not rise during the war. There were a number of charitably funded almshouses and, on the whole, families supported in this way just about avoided the stigma of pauperism if they had not appealed for help from the Board of Guardians. The Local Government Board inspector's returns for 1914 and 1915 showed Exeter's Board supported an average of fourteen registered paupers per 1,000 of the population – about 680 men, women and children – during each of those years. The figures for July 1915, for example, reveal 342 workhouse paupers, 255 paupers receiving outdoor relief, and twenty-five vagrants. To modern eyes these are large numbers, but the figures for Bideford, Holsworthy, Honiton, Okehampton, Plymouth, Plympton St Mary, South Molton, Torrington and Totnes Poor Law unions were twenty or more per 1,000, and out of the twenty Devon unions only Devonport, at thirteen, was lower than Exeter.

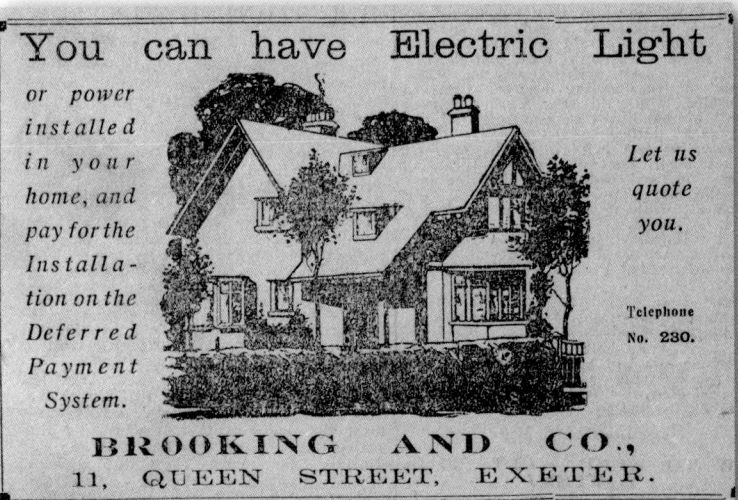

Advertisement for electric lighting. (Trewman's Flying Post, 9.1.15)

Advertisement for cooking by gas. (Trewman's Flying Post, 25.4.14)

The High Street contained a number of high-class shops, notably in Eastgate Parade. In 1914, Barns & Van Houtens was especially proud of its new millinery department to which 'a visit of inspection is invited'. And at Messrs Walton & Company's innovative High Street arcade citizens could admire nineteen windows displaying 'costumes, blouses, millinery, ladies and children's outfitting, and footwear' without worrying about the weather, and then enjoy refreshments in the 'cosy tearoom'.

The city streets remained busy and at times uncomfortable. In 1915 traders complained, although they should not have been surprised, that visitor numbers, especially from America, had declined, but no doubt the significant influx of troops more than compensated in numbers if not in wealth. As we have seen, there had been considerable dissatisfaction with aspects of the city centre before the war. In 1912, by-laws had finally banned the numerous handcarts covered with advertisements for shops and services that littered, and often blocked, the narrow streets, and it became an offence to throw bottles and broken glass, 'orange peels,

The High Street Arcade. (Dr Sadru Bhanji)

Exeter High Street; the Guildhall protrudes on the left. (Author's collection)

banana skins or any other dangerous substances' onto the roads. Nevertheless, although hotly debated, the incessant but traditional ringing of bells, clanging of gongs, and shouting to attract custom was allowed to continue.

In 1915, Exeter's chief constable remarked on the increasing congestion in Queen Street, with so many motor vehicles and carriages passing along it per hour. In the last twelve months, 118 people had been injured on the city's streets, and he fumed that motorists stopped where they liked and then left their cars unattended. Nothing was done, and although in June 1916 the city council debated

A NIGHT OUT

The Devon historian W.G. Hoskins said that just before the war an evening out for two could be had for 1/6½d. 'Two seats at the music hall or theatre cost 1s (1s 6d if one was trying to make an impression) a packet of cigarettes 2d, a glass of beer 1½d, and a glass of port for the lady 3d. If supper followed … then a plate of sausage and mash cost 4d and a really expensive meal was steak and chips at 1s 6d.' A police constable or labourer on 25/- a week, or even a carpenter, plumber or bricklayer on 35/-, might well think twice about the meal.

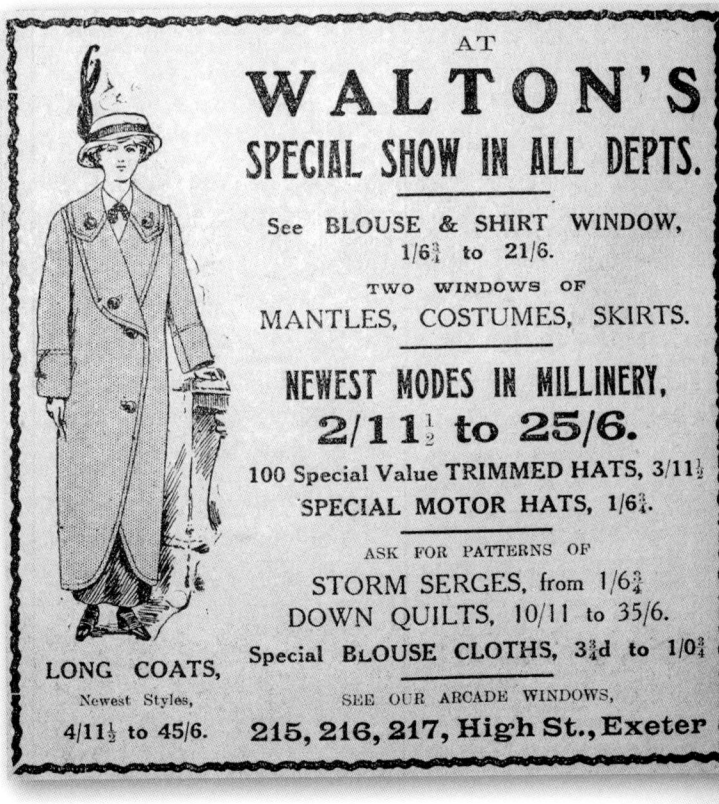

AT
WALTON'S
SPECIAL SHOW IN ALL DEPTS.

See BLOUSE & SHIRT WINDOW,
1/6¾ to 21/6.

TWO WINDOWS OF
MANTLES, COSTUMES, SKIRTS.

NEWEST MODES IN MILLINERY,
2/11½ to 25/6.

100 Special Value TRIMMED HATS, 3/11½
SPECIAL MOTOR HATS, 1/6¾.

ASK FOR PATTERNS OF
STORM SERGES, from 1/6¾
DOWN QUILTS, 10/11 to 35/6.

Special BLOUSE CLOTHS, 3¾d to 1/0¾

LONG COATS,
Newest Styles,
4/11½ to 45/6.

SEE OUR ARCADE WINDOWS,
215, 216, 217, High St., Exeter

Walton's advertisement. (Trewman's Flying Post, 3.10.14)

PAUPERS & THE POOR LAW
The 1834 Poor Law Amendment Act obliged parishes to group together to form Poor Law unions and create workhouses for the cost-effective relief of paupers. Conditions were kept Spartan to deter applicants and reduce costs, and inmates endured strict discipline, separation from their families and wore special uniforms. Although the growth of Friendly Societies and pre-war welfare reforms mitigated poverty, in 1914 the Poor Law institutions remained full as the last resort of the destitute.

stopping traders selling goods from 'trucks or barrows' between 10 a.m. and 7 p.m. on weekdays from Exe Bridge to Paris Street, and also along the High Street end of most adjoining roads, the motion failed as public safety was considered less important than local commerce. The same meeting considered banning perambulators between 11 a.m. and 5 p.m. on Fridays between the Mint and London Inn Square, but again the needs of commerce triumphed. However, the indignation of some members at a recent survey showing 312 prams cluttering the High Street 'with its atmosphere laden with dust and germs' meant the proposal only failed by twenty-two votes to twenty.

Exeter possessed a substantial number of middle-class families. They tended to live in the elegant eighteenth-century town houses of tree-lined Southernhay East and West, and Bedford Circus and Dix's Field to the east and south of the cathedral, or the large late nineteenth and early twentieth century houses of Mount Radford, Denmark Road, Spicer Road, Baring Crescent, St Leonard's Road and Lyndhurst Road a little further south. Here lived many of the city's solicitors, doctors, clergymen, bankers, merchants, company directors, and retired gentlemen – no doubt some of them ex-colonial administrators, civil servants and army or navy officers. Just before the outbreak of war the middle-class houses of Thornton Hill in St Davids had been completed, and the famous Veitch's Nurseries not far away were in the hands of developers.

Properties a little less substantial lined the western part of Polsloe Road and some short roads branching off it, while in the later years of Queen Victoria's reign and throughout that of King Edward VII, large artisan estates full of terraced houses had been erected each side of Okehampton Street to the west of the river and adjoining the Old Tiverton Road leading out of the city to the east. Much of the land in the south between

Sidwell Street and Heavitree Road was turned into the terraced streets of Newtown. They could be rented for about £13 a year. Numbered in thousands, these sturdy and comfortable houses possessed a sitting room, kitchen, parlour and several bedrooms together with a coal house, toilet and small garden. They were a massive improvement upon the ancient and overcrowded lathe-and-plaster tenements littering parts of St Paul's and St John's Wards in the west of the city, not far from the numerous factories and workshops on Exe Island and Shilhay.

In February 1913, the city council discussed its medical officer's alarming report on the West Quarter's tenements with their dark, rickety staircases, tiny partitioned rooms, poor light and ventilation, crumbling walls and ceilings, and deplorable sanitary conditions. After a heated debate, some members toured the district but a subsequent council meeting decided that, although a few tenements needed improving, by and large the lives of the 724 inhabitants were in no great danger. Perhaps it was no coincidence that in April, Alderman John Stocker, chairman of the education committee, secured £40 on a council vote to provide a summer holiday school at the County Ground in St Thomas, embracing nature walks, country dancing, story telling, choral singing and team games for children living in 'the miserable squalid surroundings of a poor district'. The *Flying Post* reported that 160 children attended, with many others looking enviously through the railings. It was held again in August 1914, just as the city mobilised for war. Soup kitchens were sometimes needed when families on the edge of making ends meet suffered as a result of even a relatively slight downturn in the local economy – as in 1907–08, again in the winter of 1909–10, and during the later railway strikes. A hesitant start on clearing the dark courts, sunless rooms and foul alleyways of Paul Street was made in 1910.

The weeks before the outbreak of war witnessed a number of spectacular events in the city. Two key ones unashamedly celebrated the greatness of the nation. On 27 June, the County Ground hosted a popular Military Tattoo, with 'striking gymnastic exercises' and 'special riding and jumping events', with music provided by the pipers and drummers of the Gordon

Bedford Circus.
(Dr Sadru Bhanji)

Highlanders and the band of the Royal 1st Devon Yeomanry. And in the last week of July, the city's 25th annual carnival was eagerly awaited. The chosen theme was Exeter and Devon's central roles in the creation of the British Empire. A host of city firms and clubs created the colourful tableaux:

Messrs Ross	Sir Francis Drake at prayer before sailing the South Seas.
Devon & Somerset Stores	Sir Francis Drake and Sultan Baber.
Exeter Cycling Club	Sir John Hawkins bringing news of Drake's success.
Messrs Colsons	Queen Elizabeth aboard the *Golden Hind.*
Messrs Ross	Sir Walter Raleigh laying down his cloak before Queen Elizabeth.
Exeter Tourers Cycling Club	The news of the Spanish Armada reaches Devon.
Willey & Co.	Raleigh on board the *Madre de Dios.*
Exeter Rovers	The boyhood of Raleigh as painted by Millais (in nearby Budleigh Salterton).

Tramway staff	Queen Elizabeth boxes the Earl of Essex (her favourite) on the ears.
Exeter YMCA	Captain Scott's dash for the pole (the previous December Commander Evans from Scott's expedition had given two slide lectures at a packed Victoria Hall).
Exeter YMCA	Captain Oates going to his death.
Exeter Harriers Athletics Club	The last moments of Sir Humphrey Gilbert (his ship, the *Squirrel*, foundered off Newfoundland, the colony he had just secured).

Soon afterwards the final peacetime summer events were hosted in and around the city. On 29 July there was beautiful weather for Heavitree and District's extensive Horticultural and Cottage Garden Show, during which the dashing 'boy' aviator Marcus Manton amazed the crowds with his aerial acrobatics. The following day the sun shone equally brightly on the Cottage Garden Show in the grounds of Haldon House, the home of the Bannatyne family, and on 31 July a Flower Show graced Broadclyst, a village owned by the influential Acland family of nearby Killerton House. On 3 August the threat of gloomy weather did not spoil the Flower Show at Whipton or the Conservative Garden Party at 'Maryfield', the city home of Exeter's MP, Henry Duke. Cheap tickets for railway excursions had been suddenly withdrawn for that day, but the bank holiday trains from Exeter to Exmouth, Dawlish, Teignmouth and Okehampton were crowded despite the full fares being charged.

The following day, on 4 August, war was declared and the weather was grey, windy and wet. A host of seaside regattas, sporting events and other fetes and shows were cancelled, the seaside paddle-steamers were requisitioned by the Royal Navy for conversion to gunboats and minesweepers, and the proprietors of hotels and guest houses bemoaned the cancelled bookings.

ENGLAND AND EXETER IN 1914

In 1914 Exeter seemed to epitomise the unchanging calm and confidence of pre-war Great Britain. Its ancient cathedral was its greatest building, its large townhouses were occupied by the city's mercantile, ecclesiastical, legal and medical elite, and the city lay amidst undulating countryside dominated by the mansions and estates of aristocrats and baronets. It was as though the Barchester of Anthony Trollope's celebrated novels had sprung to life.

However Devon, much like Barchester, was undergoing remorseless change. In 1914, it had just about recovered from a deep agricultural depression caused by importing cheap North American grain. A dramatic, and painful, switch from largely arable farming to animal husbandry had saved the day. Fortunately, the local railway network had nearly reached its maximum extent and now took huge quantities of beef, fruit and vegetables out of the county and brought thousands of tourists in. The county was not nearly as static as its huddled villages, sweeping landed estates and popular seaside resorts might have seemed. And the great warships sailing in and out of Devonport reminded everyone that there was a mighty empire to defend.

Family life was changing. Mass production and the retail revolution were providing families with a previously unheard of array of household goods – at all sorts of prices. Mass education, another late Victorian invention, was giving all children a grounding in reading, writing and arithmetic, and ensured they understood the need to live God-fearing lives in the service of their fellow men, especially their employers. Families who could afford fees much preferred the independent private and grammar schools. Poverty was allevi-ated largely by charity, with the Poor Law acting as an unpalatable safety net, and like many cities Exeter possessed almshouses and hospitals founded and supported by private benefactions. In diverse ways, the distinctions of social class still remained readily identifiable and most Devon people rarely questioned their ingrained habits of natural superiority or deference.

Queen Street station. (Author's collection)

2

PREPARATIONS AT HOME

Over the August bank holiday of 1914, the 3,371 officers and men of the 4th, 5th and 6th Territorial battalions of the Devons and 4th and 5th Territorial battalions of the Duke of Cornwall's Light Infantry (the Cornwalls) continued training amidst the squalls sweeping across the heathland of Woodbury Common between Exeter and Exmouth. There was a great deal of checking and cleaning equipment, marching and parading, preparing messages and signalling, and making mock attacks on defended outposts. There were also well-attended Church of England, Wesleyan and Roman Catholic services. Two days later, the men broke camp and marched the 12 miles to Exeter St David's station accompanied by numerous steam lorries and lumbering horse wagons, many of them requisitioned from local breweries. Amidst cheering crowds, the men, horses and vast arrays of equipment boarded trains for Plymouth and garrison duty along the coast.

The *Flying Post* noted that as they passed through Exeter the Devons were cheered louder than the Cornwalls, and the 4th Devons, composed mainly of city men, was cheered loudest of all. 'The Brigade had had its first taste of hard soldiering,' said the *Western Morning News*, 'and made not a murmur of complaint.' This is unlikely. Earl Fortescue, the very active colonel of the Devons and also the county's Lord Lieutenant, was appalled by the men's hungry and uncomfortable night on the train and their lack of breakfast in Plymouth before the long, hot, and dusty marches to outlying fortresses. He fumed at the officers' incompetence. The regimental history also remarks upon the frightening inadequacy of clothing and equipment in all the battalions in 1914, something Fortescue worked hard to successfully remedy, partly through local contractors.

A few days later, Private May's diary records the supreme importance soldiers attached to the food they received. When he arrived at Exeter's Queen Street station from Topsham Barracks, he was given lemonade, a sandwich, an apple and packet of Woodbine cigarettes, at Salisbury he got tea, and at Larkhill Camp that evening he enjoyed bread, cheese and more tea.

As the local men started to leave the city, life became more regimented for everyone. A few days after war was declared, the Defence of the Realm Act was passed, allowing the government to impose the regulations it wanted upon national life through the speedy mechanism of Orders in Council. It was used to control everything from the requisition of buildings, the protection of military sites and the banning of lights, to the censorship of newspaper reports, the restrictions on licensed premises and the control of food production and prices. The acronym DORA lent itself to the Act being portrayed as a pinched-faced, mean-spirited interfering spin-ster, but despite some unnecessarily pettifogging regulations, such as potential imprisonment for wasting scraps of bread, it contributed significantly to the government's ability to respond quickly to a host of wartime problems. The mocking cartoons did not necessarily invalidate the wartime need for tight centralised controls.

As early as September 1914, a local newspaper contained warnings to motorists that they might be stopped at any time, but especially at night, by troops guarding coastal roads and mili-tary facilities. It cautioned drivers to take great care, especially on corners, in case troops were out on manoeuvres. No head-lights were to be used on any roads along the coast – the fears of suspected spies and signals to enemy vessels loomed large in Devon throughout the war. Be warned, said the *Flying Post*, that the noise of a motor vehicle's engine could easily drown the

HOW · TO · WIN · THE · WAR!

Cartoon mocking the effect of DORA. Asquith is in the wheelchair being pushed by Lloyd George. (Trewman's Flying Post, 30.10.15)

sound of the sentry's challenge, with fatal consequences. Indeed, in January 1915, two officers were shot dead by a jittery sentry along the seafront in Torquay when they objected to his order to stop and prove their identities.

A few days after the declaration of war, Lord Fortescue chaired a public meeting in Exeter to co-ordinate Devon's response to the emergency. Although a Patriotic Fund and a clothing collection were started to tide poor families over any immediate problems, and appeals made to more affluent residents not to hoard food, Fortescue's immediate concern was to counter the numerous spies and saboteurs who were believed to have infiltrated the county before the war. Railway junctions, signal boxes and tunnels and bridges were especially vulnerable, and as a stopgap he urged those who lived near them to keep a close watch 'and if he had with him a strong gun and a dog who disliked strangers it would be no harm, and to take any steps up to shooting to keep at a distance those who were evilly disposed'. Within a few days Boy Scouts were employed on railway and coastal watches and were much praised for their diligence. In due course, railway staff, police and servicemen took over the security of the important lines for troop movements – all of which came through the main railway junctions in Exeter.

In October the governors of Exeter's higher education establishment, the Royal Albert Memorial College, were faced with rapidly spreading accusations that it was harbouring two enemy aliens who might well be spies. They were identified as two tutors, Mr Sager and Mr Schoop. The former turned out to be the son of émigré Russian parents and had been born in Sheffield fifty years ago, and the latter had left Germany in 1895 and taken British citizenship in 1901. The fear of German spies was long lasting, largely because government propaganda, paranoid

HUGH FORTESCUE, 4TH EARL FORTESCUE (1854–1932)
A typical late Victorian paternal aristocrat, Fortescue was Harrow and Cambridge educated, and a local Liberal MP before succeeding his father in 1905. From his Castle Hill estate at Filleigh, he became master of the Devon & Somerset Staghounds, colonel of the County Territorials, chairman of Devon County Council (1904–16), and Lord Lieutenant (1903–28). As Lord Lieutenant he threw himself into wartime efforts to improve recruitment, agriculture and security.

articles in the newspapers, and alarmist novels such as William Le Queux's *The Invasion of 1910* and John Buchan's *The Thirty Nine Steps* kept anger and suspicions at fever pitch. But real spies did exist. A sensational trial occurred in Exeter when Max Schulz, a German officer, was caught masquerading as a newspaper reporter in Plymouth in 1911. And throughout the war German submarines prowled the Devon coast.

Earl and Countess Fortescue. (Devon Heritage Centre)

The Royal Albert Memorial Museum. It housed the School of Art and Science, which grew into the Royal Albert Memorial College in neighbouring Gandy Street. (Dr Sadru Bhanji)

Aerial attack was feared too. In January 1915, the city decided to reduce public lighting and residents had to ensure no domestic lights could be seen from the outside. The announcement said:

> On receipt of warning of the approach of enemy aircraft, the supply of gas and electricity will be cut off at the respective works. A succession of sharp blasts will be sounded by the hooter at Messrs Willey's work, St Thomas.

Citizens were urged to take refuge indoors, preferably in cellars.

One official anxiety was perhaps mitigated by the publicity given to the request of the commanding officer at Higher Barracks: that citizens should not treat reservists or volunteers with intoxicating drinks on their departure to the barracks or railway station. Nevertheless, quite a few soldiers appeared in court for being drunk, although they were usually dismissed into the army's custody without a fine, unless they were on leave. In one case, a Welshmen in the Devons amused the Bench by claiming he had been surprised by the strength of Exeter beer compared with that brewed in the Rhonda Valley. In November 1914, the city's magistrates prohibited the sale of alcohol after 9.30 p.m. on weekdays and 9.00 p.m. on Sundays, and the local army commander forbade soldiers from entering licensed premises from 6.00 a.m. until 12.00 p.m. unless they possessed proof that they had been on night duty.

Exeter's retailers leapt equally quickly into action. As early as 8 August, Warren Bros offered special prices to officers wishing to avail themselves of storage facilities. Soon afterwards, Collins & Son, military tailors, advertised that they stocked 'every requisite for full and undress wear and camp equipment' for every branch of the armed forces, and T. Evins & Co. in the High Street reassured officers that it was the official manufacturer of 'Wolseley' sleeping valises, sleeping bags and kit bags. John Guest in the High Street was quick to advertise his stock of the words and music for all the Allied national anthems.

After all the controversy surrounding the suffragettes, Mrs Pankhurst's return to the city as a free and much feted woman in November 1914 must have surprised, gratified and frightened people in about equal measure. At a meeting at the Palladium, replete with the Devons' band and patriotic songs, she confirmed that the suffrage campaign took second place to the war effort and asserted that all men should enlist and all women should take their place in the city's shops, offices and workshops. Equally authoritatively, she stated that 'the fact of invasion was one they should look full in the face'. 'A good many men,' she argued, 'were afraid of what would happen to their business. That was a wrong view, for they might, before long, have no business at all to attend to.'

Exeter's Anglican clergy were also very much aware of wartime pressures and saw them as an opportunity for spiritual regeneration as much as an immediate crisis that they must help to resolve. The city's parish churches and cathedral held regular and, at least to start with, well-attended intercessions. In April 1915, the *Flying Post* claimed that families across the city were drawing a degree of comfort and pride from the rolls of honour naming parish volunteers that were read out at services and from the peace bells that sounded in churches at 12.00 p.m. every day. However, as an earlier report revealed, the *Flying Post* knew only too well that the decision to read out the names was more about shaming others into enlisting than honouring those already serving.

Ross' advertisement.
(Trewman's Flying
Post, 5.9.14)

John Guest's
advertisement.
(Trewman's Flying
Post, 15.8.14)

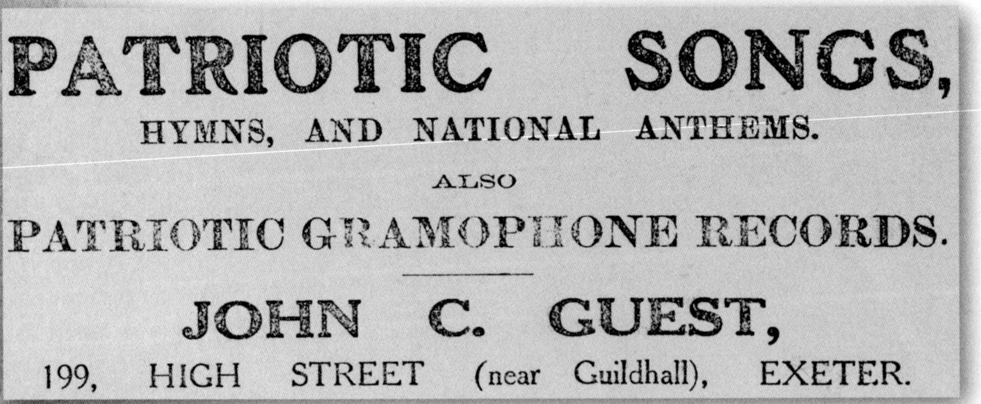

The diocese was keenly aware that there were 40,000 extra servicemen in Devon – several thousand of them in Exeter – and that relatively few might be regular worshippers. The clergy visited the war hospitals regularly and a series of denominational and interdenominational men's clubs offering games, books, magazines, refreshments and like-minded company and support prospered as never before. In January 1925, one city clergyman asserted that 'the war was like a flame that tested the strength of a building it ignited, and the Church of England was there to give that strength'. The moral health of the city was another consideration as the number of visiting servicemen soared. As early as December 1914, Exeter's chief constable welcomed the decision of the National Union of Women Workers to work alongside the police in arranging street patrols 'in the interests of young girls'.

The Exeter Diocesan Association for the Care of Girls, generally known as St Olave's Trust, was founded in 1879. Its aim was to offer temporary refuge to 'friendless' girls, women 'in moral danger' and to those already immersed in 'an immoral way of life'. It gave them spiritual and vocational training, generally as domestic servants, and found many of them places of work. The Trust cared for single mothers during the latter stages of pregnancy and placed their babies in foster homes. It worked in conjunction with the House of Mercy at Bovey Tracey where longer-term spiritual, moral and vocational training took place, and also with the Church Temperance Society's home for inebriate women in the city. By 1914, St Olave's work was centred at Nos 32 and 33 Bartholomew Street East, and it was kept busy. In 1913, eighty-eight girls were admitted, and a year later the Trust feared it would be busier still as the war dislocated families by drawing girls away from home to work, and men away to camps and billets. It was right. Numbers rose to over 100, and the refuge and maternity home were often full. In 1914, twenty girls had to be refused admission and in 1915 a record sixty babies were boarded out.

The war immediately deprived the city's pauper children of a new home just outside the workhouse. Exeter's Board of Guardians had opened a new purpose-built children's home in Heavitree Road in February 1914. The Guardians had decided against the 'scattered homes' option adopted by those in Newton Abbot and Plymouth, whereby a small group of orphans lived in ordinary-looking houses with a supervising and training matron. Instead, Exeter's Guardians thought that the fifty boys and girls living in the new home would still experience a family like atmosphere and the cost would not be nearly as great. They equipped the home with a large laundry and cooking range so the girls could receive practical training as domestic servants and further cut the cost to ratepayers. And, the *Flying Post* was pleased to learn, the girls also would scrub the floors. In the event these carefully laid plans had to be deferred when, a few months later, the large new building was deemed particularly suitable for use as an emergency war hospital.

The large modern building housing the prestigious Episcopal Girls' School, just past the railway bridge where Longbrook Street leads to Pennsylvania, was also immediately requisitioned as a war hospital. The classes were quickly found alternative homes elsewhere across the city. Other immediate signs of war included the order for families and businesses to take the horses they owned to Higher Barracks, where many were purchased by the army. The Highland Light Infantry's Territorial battalions arrived and took over St Sidwell's School, and soon afterwards St James' School was also requisitioned for billets. A little later St Luke's Teachers' Training College in Heavitree Road, together with part

The Children's Home in Heavitree, requisitioned as Number 3 War Hospital. (Dr Sadru Bhanji)

*Episcopal Modern
School for Girls.
(Author's collection)*

of the city workhouse opposite it, became the wartime base for
over 250 clerks of the Army Pay Corps. Over the next few years,
many local women and older men were employed as ancillaries
and additional office workers there. St Luke's numbers were
decimated when students rushed to join the army and several
tutors sailed to India as officers in the Territorials. Tutor's letters
from camps at Ferozepore and Amritsar suggest that numerous
rugby, cricket and soccer matches relieved the general boredom.

In contrast, when the early casualties arrived in the city they
brought with them terrible stories of German atrocities and
editors were quick to print their tales of wounded and helpless British soldiers being bayonetted, captured soldiers being
crucified on barn doors, Belgian children being found with
their hands and feet cut off, and the gruesome sight of whole
families massacred and mutilated. Not surprisingly, in April 1915,
the *Flying Post* thought it apposite to reprint a vituperative
article from the *Daily Mail* urging the complete subjugation of
Germany, arguing that it had never honoured any agreements or
treaties it had signed. It declared, 'We might as well offer buns to
a python,' for the German people were forever ready to 'drench
half the world with blood'. It concluded: 'We can only hope to
give them such a thrashing that it will be generations before they
again seek to fulfil their tragic destiny.' Many people agreed, but
despite the horrors, local recruitment figures disappointed the
civil and military authorities.

ATROCITIES

Historians agree that British propaganda, and soldiers' stories, citing German atrocities in Belgium knowingly enhanced the horrors, but nevertheless they existed. Historian David Stevenson notes the wilful destruction of ancient Louvain and Ypres, and states German soldiers' diaries, Belgian refugees' reports and the 'more sober' Allied inquiries suggest that 5,500 Belgian and 900 French civilians were deliberately killed in the initial German advance.

Senior clergy reinforced the image of Germany as evil incarnate and newspapers made much of their sermons and addresses. From the cathedral pulpit on Easter Sunday 1915, the Right Revd Archibald Robertson, bishop of Exeter, said, 'Today we are confronted, not with war only, but with hatred; pent-up, cold calculated hatred, which imparted to warfare the horror of unchristian savagery.' We must fight ardently against evil, he asserted, but 'honourably' as true Christian warriors. His suffragan, the Right Revd Robert Trefusis, bishop of Crediton, a resident of the Cathedral Close and grandson of Lord Clinton, was equally clear which nation occupied the high moral ground. Germany was the Antichrist, he thundered in the cathedral in early 1915. It was 'the destroyer of peace, the murderer of the aged and the helpless, the outrager

The Rt Revd Archibald Robertson, Lord Bishop of Exeter from 1903–16. (Devon and Exeter Institution)

The Rt Revd Robert Trefusis, Bishop of Crediton from 1897–1930. (Devon and Exeter Institution)

of women, the devastator of villages and towns and sacred buildings – cruel, barbaric, tyrannical'. It was every Christian's duty to take up arms against it.

Unfortunately, by spring 1915, as the bishops knew well, local recruitment rates had plummeted. For a short time the height and fitness standards had been raised when the recruiting stations and barracks were overwhelmed by the early clamour to enlist, but soon they had to be lowered again. Within a month of the outbreak of war there were worries that enlistment across the city and county was flagging. In Exeter there were 434 recruits up to 22 August 1914, and the *Flying Post* regretted 'that exaggerated reports' about recruitment had been published. At the end of August, a sermon by Canon McLaren at the cathedral bemoaned the widely varying rates of volunteering across the nation's towns and villages. In a barely concealed indictment of local efforts, he called upon local politicians of all parties to 'bring home the urgency of the need, and the obligations of patriotism to the men who are still only half awake'. Around this time Lord Fortescue, assisted by Lord Clinton, Lord Clifford of Chudleigh and Sir Ian Amory of Knightshayes, established an Exeter-based Parliamentary Recruiting Committee that energetically cajoled town mayors and local councils into literally 'banging the drum' around their streets to shame laggards and stiffen recruitment.

The Committee kept careful records of local efforts, but in November 1914 Lord Fortescue did not hide his dismay. Up to the beginning of that month, not counting local men who were in the regular army and navy at the outbreak of war, Devon had provided 5,000 men for territorial battalions and 5,000 men for regular army and navy units. In November, recruitment across the county averaged 400 a week. It was not good enough, the Lord Lieutenant announced. It represented just 0.6% of the population, whereas Gloucestershire had managed 1.39%, Dorset 1.44%, Birmingham 3.35% and Warwickshire 4.07%. Fortescue noted that a few patriotic Devon communities had achieved a magnificent 10%, but many others had failed abysmally to respond to the country's needs. He emphasised that Field Marshal Earl Kitchener, the Secretary of State for War, now sought 1 million more men, and as 6% of the population was the estimated target, this meant that Devon had to produce 40,000 recruits. Fortescue, though, claimed that the parish returns to his committee revealed that there were 50,000 men in Devon aged 18–35, not counting those unfit, and therefore another 37,000 recruits were there to be found. At an important Recruiting Committee meeting in the Guildhall in December 1914, the mayor felt Exeter was being unfairly criticised, possibly more by implication than direct accusation, and asserted that 'he was not prepared to admit that the city had done badly in the way of recruiting'. Figures showed, he claimed, that between 2,400 and 2,500 were serving in various branches of the armed forces. Fortescue was emollient, but said he had noticed many eligible men still working in the city's shops.

The hunt was intensified and a series of well-organised recruiting marches, complete with an officer, a couple of dozen soldiers, a military band, and an experienced public speaker, usually an MP, toured the towns and villages of Devon throughout 1915. Exeter was not exempt. There was plenty of pre-visit publicity and local councillors, clergy and schools were expected to ensure the largest possible audience turned out. Across the county the soldiers enjoyed warm welcomes from the children, teachers, clergy and families from the 'big house', and were plied with plentiful food and drink, but they also encountered surly silence, muttered insults and downright hostility from many residents and their families. On occasion, the soldiers were taunted into hostile responses and overall the number of recruits gleaned from the intensive week-long marches across the length and breadth of Devon in 1915 was about 400 men, hardly commensurate with the effort. The results do, however, confirm the conclusions of historians such as David Stevenson that the southern agricultural counties were far less enthusiastic about volunteering than northern counties and the major industrial cities.

By the end of 1914 it was proving difficult to persuade any more men in Exeter to volunteer for active service. On 11 December the *Western Times* lamented that the noisy and colourful city rallies were having no effect anymore. 'Each night this week there has been a military procession watched through the principal thoroughfares by big, cheering crowds, and yet in four days fewer than a score of volunteers have come forward to join "Exeter's Own", the Company of 250 which it was hoped could be formed this week, to be attached to the 11th Battalion of the Devon Regiment.' The rallies were big events, with bands and 1,000 soldiers marching through different targeted areas of the city each time. Some were held at night and accompanied by up to 200 torchbearers.

Not surprisingly, scorn was heaped upon the eligible men staying sat home. The newspaper claimed, 'the young men of Exeter, the single young men with no domestic responsibilities, badly needed waking up to their duty in this crisis.' It imagined how shameful they would feel when their families later recalled the names of those who fought for the nation's survival. As part of the desperate attempt to boost recruitment, the Hippodrome created a large tableau under the heading 'Will they never come?' showing a British soldier, rifle in hand, standing over a wounded comrade and looking in the direction of the English shore. The tableau was set in a snow scene, just like the recent battles in Flanders.

*Cartoon 'Daddy, why weren't you a soldier?' (*Trewman's Flying Post, *27.2.15)*

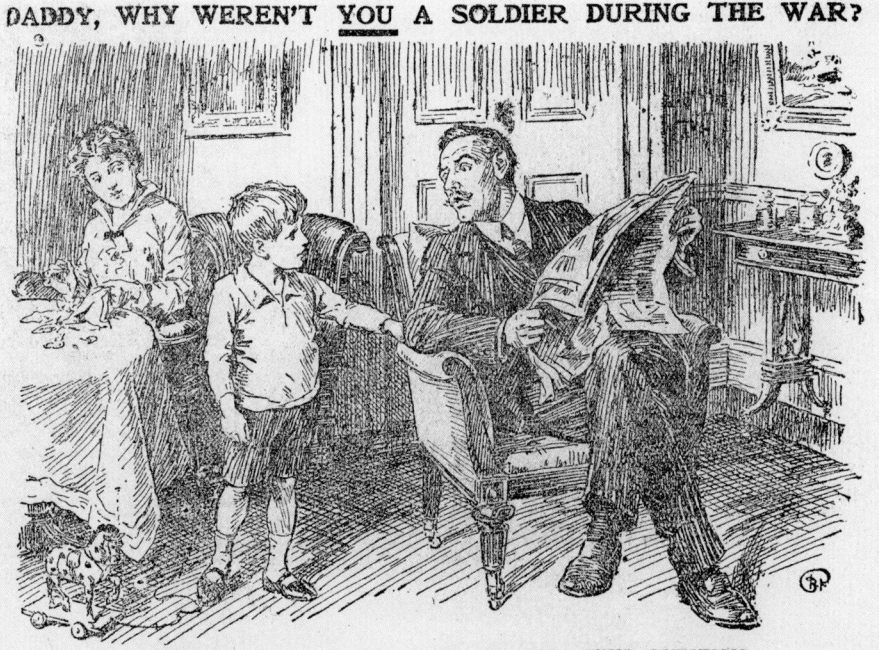

DADDY, WHY WEREN'T YOU A SOLDIER DURING THE WAR?

IN YEARS TO COME *YOU* MAY BE ASKED THIS QUESTION.
Join the Army at once, and help to secure the glorious Empire of which *your* little son will be a citizen.

Large advertisements appeared in the local newspapers. They aimed at a range of emotions but mainly, by 1915, shame and guilt at staying home. One series took the form of weekly sets of photographs of local volunteers above the inscription:

THESE BOYS DIDN'T SHIRK

THEY WANT HELP!! Listen for a moment – can't you hear them calling TO YOU?
BE A MAN There's a king's uniform waiting for YOU.
Go and put it on NOW!

GOD SAVE THE KING!!!

Another blatantly targeted pride in a mighty but beneficent British Empire:

An Englishman's Catechism

WHO made this little Island the greatest and most powerful Empire the world has ever seen?
Our forefathers

WHO ruled this Empire with such wisdom and sympathy that every part of it – of whatever race or religion – has rallied to it in its hour of need?
Our fathers

WHO will stand up to preserve this great and glorious heritage?
We will

WHO will remember us with pride and exultation and thankfulness if we do our duty today?
Our Children

ENLIST TO-DAY
GOD SAVE THE KING

A third came far closer to home and attempted to arouse thoughts of family and public scorn and personal self-contempt:

YOUNG MAN

Is anyone proud of you?

Is your **mother** proud of you?
Is your **sister** proud of you?
Is your **sweetheart** proud of you?
Is your **employer** proud of you?
Is your **Country** proud of you?

If you are not making munitions,
get into khaki to-day and
they will all be proud of you.

In October 1915, one of the last recruiting marches and rallies took place in Exeter. After the singing of 'Land of Hope and Glory', Brigadier General Lord St Levan, commanding officer of the Devon and Cornwall Territorials, Lieutenant Colonel Kirkwood, commanding officer of the Devons's Depot, and James Owen, the mayor, tried to rouse the crowd, but Owen noted the absence of men of military age. He urged mothers, wives and sweethearts to persuade their menfolk to enlist, but a woman in front of him merely laughed. Clearly angered, he replied that he hoped it would be a very different matter if we had been overrun, like Belgium and Poland. And he went on to say that if the rallies failed, as this one obviously did, 'there were other means' by which the men could be brought to the front line. Conscription was now very much in the air.

THE WARTIME EXPANSION OF THE DEVONS

In summer 1914 there were three battalions; four years later there were twenty-one plus five labour, works and home garrison battalions.

Regular Army

1st Battalion:	Western Front August 1914–November 1917, then Italy until April 1918 when it returned to France
2nd Battalion:	Egypt until October 1914 and then on the Western Front
3rd (Reserve) Battalion:	A training unit based in Exeter, Plymouth and Devonport feeding other battalions and providing Plymouth's garrison

Territorial Force

1/4th Battalion:	Exeter August 1914, then India and Mesopotamia
1/5th Battalion:	Plymouth August 1914, then India, Suez and the Western Front
1/6th Battalion:	Barnstaple August 1914, then India and Mesopotamia
1/7th (Cyclist) Battalion:	Exeter August 1914, then the North East, Suffolk and Kent
2/4th Battalion:	Formed Exeter September 1914, then India and Egypt
2/5th Battalion:	Formed Plymouth September 1914, then Egypt
2/6th Battalion:	Formed Barnstaple September 1914, then India and Mesopotamia
2/7th (Cyclist) Battalion:	Formed Totnes October 1914, then Kent and Essex
3/4th, 3/5th & 3/6th Battalions:	Formed Exeter, Plymouth and Barnstaple respectively March 1915. Later amalgamated as 4th Reserve Battalion and in Ireland April 1918

3/7th (Cyclist) Battalion:	Formed late 1915, disbanded March 1916
15th Battalion:	Formed January 1917 from a 'home service only' Territorial Battalion. In Aldeburgh 1918
16th (Royal 1st Devon & Royal North Devon Yeomanry) Battalion:	Formed January 1917 in Egypt from two dismounted Yeomanry units. In Marseilles May 1918

Battalions of the New Armies

8th (Service) Battalion:	Formed Exeter August 1914, then France and Italy
9th (Service) Battalion:	Formed Exeter September 1914, then France and Italy and back to France
10th (Service) Battalion:	Formed Exeter September 1914, then France and Salonika
11th (Reserve) Battalion:	Formed Exeter November 1914. Remained a Training and Reserve Battalion

Other Battalions

12th (Labour) Battalion:	Formed Devonport May 1916, then France
13th (Works) Battalion:	Formed Saltash June 1916, stayed in Plymouth
14th (Labour) Battalion:	Formed Plymouth August 1916, then France
1st (Garrison) Battalion:	Formed Weymouth August 1915, then Egypt and Palestine
2nd (Home Service) Garrison Battalion:	Formed Exeter July 1916, then Plymouth and Falmouth

Three training battalions – the 51st, 52nd and 53rd – were formed with notional attachment to various regiments, including the Devons.

3

WORK OF WAR

Exeter's initial fears of severe unemployment and social distress proved largely unfounded, although significant changes took place in the workforce as a result of war contracts and enlistment. In September 1914, Lord Fortescue raised Devon's Territorial Force to 6,000, and thereby provided seventeen city firms of tailors with plenty of work completing 350 uniforms a week – each one comprising underclothes, shirt, jacket, trousers, puttees, leggings, cap and greatcoat. The following March, local tailoring workshops were still at full stretch catering for the demand for underclothes and uniforms for the soldiers in local barracks or hospitals. Some bitterness had arisen between employers and their sub-contracted employees when the latter had decided to go freelance and increase their earnings, but in doing so jeopardise the commercial contracts of the workshop owners. Worries that fifty young seamstresses would be out of work when a collar factory closed early in the war due to a lack of orders were needless, as alternative work became readily available. The city council and education committee, together with private donations, helped some of the young women to acquire new tailoring skills.

In August 1915, a consortium of engineers and businessmen, including James Owen formed a new munitions company based in the Vulcan Stove Company's premises in Haven Road. Directors brought in lathes and drills from their other factories and used their own contacts and expert knowledge to secure an order for 18-pounder shell cases from the Bristol National Munitions Factory. Mr Templer Dupree, the chairman of Messrs Willey & Co., probably the largest foundry on the industrial estate, was a director of the new company and represented the linked technical and commercial interests between the two firms. Although primarily concerned with the gas industry, during the war Willey & Co. diversified to turn out a vast array of military equipment, including 1,000 aeroplane tanks, 500 mine sinkers, 7,000 cast-iron plummets for anchoring mines in the sea, 30 cast-iron engine beds for tugs, 10 tilting furnaces for melting brass, 300 back sights and 300 foresights for machine guns, 30 riveted petrol storage tanks, 3,300 pipes for use with poison gas, 60 concrete-mixing machines, 9,000 plough-shares, 100 tons of castings for harbour cranes, and several million primers and cartridges.

> **WAR PRODUCTION**
> It has been estimated that 1 mile of trenches required 900 miles of barbed wire, 6 million sandbags, 1 million cu. ft of timber, and 360,000ft of corrugated iron. By 1918 the British forces on the Western Front numbered 2.5 million men with 31,770 lorries, 7,694 cars, 3,532 ambulances, 14,464 motorcycles, 6,437 heavy guns and 1,782 aircraft.
> (Gerard J. DeGroot)

Women replaced men in a number of occupations. The *Western Times* had a picture of four city girls painting Sherborne station and being admired by wounded soldiers from the local hospital. In April 1915, the GWR employed Miss Hopping as Exeter St David's first female ticket collector, and female conductors also worked on city trams. Indeed one was on the tram that overturned on Exe Bridge in 1917 mentioned in Chapter 1. Evidence at the Exeter tribunal set up to consider the exemption of men from active service shows that by 1916 the city branches of the national Cathedral Dairy, a large wholesale woollen goods company and Heavitree Brewery had all replaced enlisted men with women in their offices and for lighter manual tasks.

Exeter's response to the army's call for the rapid establishment of fully equipped and staffed emergency hospitals was immediate and effective, not least because the Devon branch of the Red Cross and its Voluntary Aid Detachments (VADs) were extremely well prepared. From 1909, when VADs were first created, the county director, J.S.C. Davis, and his deputy, Miss Georgiana Buller, had

Doing Men's Work Wins Tommy's Approval.

THE above are four young lady painters—all Exeter girls—who are at present engaged in putting a little colour and freshness into Sherborne Railway Station. The wounded soldiers in Sherborne Hospital are much interested in the work the young ladies are doing. The fair painters are Miss Alice Slack, Miss Flossie Worth, Miss Lily Discombe, and Miss Milly Robinson.

*Women workers from Exeter employed in painting Sherborne station. (*Western Times*, 19.10.17)*

worked with ten regional assistant directors to cover the county with well-trained local detachments comprising qualified and trainee nurses and a host of support staff, including some men working as orderlies, drivers and stretcher bearers. Everything was managed from the headquarters in Exeter. In May 1914, a huge exercise was held along the coast from Exeter to Bridport to show how quickly several hundred casualties incurred defending the area from invasion could be treated and if necessary rushed to hospital. This is not to say, of course, that the director and his staff had an inkling of the enormity of the task that actually presented itself a few months later.

Number 1 War Emergency Hospital was created on 4 October 1914, and as it took over the building and facilities of the West of England Eye Infirmary it was able to receive its first casualties three days later. A *Western Times* reporter visited it just before it opened and noted the spotless operating theatre, wards and counterpanes, the individual lockers, games room and garden, and the fine view from the officers' ward. When the first trains arrived at Queen Street station from Southampton Docks with a hundred or more casualties, large crowds gathered to cheer the men. Some men waved back, but others were hardly aware of what was happening as the doctors, nurses and orderlies transferred them to the waiting cars and ambulances. Arrivals soon became routine events, however, and attracted little public attention.

The Royal Devon and Exeter Infirmary in Southernhay was not requisitioned and stayed open for civilian patients. Number 2 War Emergency Hospital was established in the large Episcopal Modern School for Girls and its first patients arrived on 16 October 1914. Its large rooms made satisfactory wards, its art room became the operating theatre and its cookery room made a serviceable kitchen. Two marquees were erected in the grounds for patients needing open-air treatment. The Children's Home in Heavitree Road became Number 3 Hospital on 31 October and a large block at Topsham Barracks (in Exeter's Barrack Road, not Topsham itself) became Number 4 Hospital in February 1915. These two hospitals catered for sick men from the large wartime garrisons in the city as well as for casualties shipped home from the Western Front.

Exeter Eye Infirmary, requisitioned as Number 1 War Hospital. (Dr Sadru Bhanji)

Building at Topsham Barracks requisitioned as Number 4 War Hospital. (Dr Sadru Bhanji)

In response to further demands, the South West College Hostel for Women and the Congregational church schools on the approach road to Rougemont Castle were turned into Number 5 Hospital in May 1915. At that date the five hospitals provided 1,170 beds. The Bishop's Palace and Streatham Hall (on the present university site) were later added as hospitals for officers. A senior medical officer was in charge of each hospital, but strictly subject to the VAD director, or, in practice, the dynamic Georgiana Buller who soon assumed the role of assistant director for Exeter as well as overall deputy director. Each hospital had a matron and fully trained nurses in a ratio of seven or eight to each 100 beds, who were supported by VAD assistants with varying degrees of nursing training and experience. Other VAD workers looked after equipment, linen and meals, and charwomen, some voluntary, did most of the cleaning.

Exeter's hospitals were front-line ones, alongside the smaller front-line ones in Torquay Town Hall and later in Newton Abbot, Sidmouth, Stoodley Knowle and Uplyme. On arrival in Devon, the sick and wounded men were taken to a front-line hospital for examination and treatment and, when deemed to be on the road to recovery, they were transferred to one of more than forty second-line voluntary convalescent hospitals across the county.

The hospitals received a capitation grant from the army but it fell far short of covering anything but the basic medical care and rations. As a consequence, huge efforts were made by local communities to ensure the hospitals received constant donations of money, food

College Hospital for Women in Castle Street requisitioned as Number 5 War Hospital. (Dr Sadru Bhanji)

and clothing. Fetes, sales, street collections and concerts on behalf of the 'Soldiers' Comforts Fund' abounded in the city throughout the year. In October 1916, a typical concert at Exeter's Victoria Hall included the popular favourites Sullivan's 'In Memoriam', Tchaikovsky's 'Reverie', 'Softly Awakes My Heart' from Saint Saen's 'Samson & Delilah' and selections from 'Yeoman of the Guard'.

The citizens of Exeter would have seen many convoys of cars and ambulances with wounded soldiers going to and from the war hospitals and the stations, but other convoys headed to more pleasurable entertainments within and beyond the city. The villages of Bradninch and Broadclyst, a few miles outside Exeter, regularly entertained wounded soldiers from the city with games on their greens and teas and concerts in their halls and marquees. From time to time, wealthy patrons and town committees invited large parties of 100 or more to days out in Teignmouth and Torquay or to picnics on Dartmoor. In August 1917, Exeter's Cycling Club entertained 250 soldiers with games and races and a revue at the Theatre Royal. Concerts in

DEVON'S WAR EMERGENCY HOSPITALS
The forty second-line hospitals were primarily for convalescence. Some of these were established in local cottage hospitals – such as Axminster, Brixham and Dartmouth, but most were in mansions handed over – not requisitioned – by wealthy county families for the duration. These included Bicton, in East Budleigh (Lord Clinton), Flete, near Ivybridge (Colonel Mildmay MP), Upottery Manor, near Honiton (Dowager Viscountess Sidmouth), Ryall's Court, near Seaton (Sir Frederick de la Pole) and Knightshayes, near Tiverton (Sir Ian Amory).

Tommy's Inevitable Fag.

A PRETTY incident at the recent Exeter Cycling Club's sports and entertainment to wounded soldiers at the St. Thomas County Grounds. Miss Mary Mead, the little daughter of the captain of the Club, distributed cigarettes among the guests, and in the above snapshot, taken by Mr. W. J. Allen, of the E.C.C. committeemen, a wounded Tommy of fine physique is seen accepting one from her tray. This particular guest, by the way, was among the competitors in the race for men with crutches, which was organised at the express wish of the wounded, and in which some of them displayed remarkable dexterity.

'Tommy's Inevitable Fag'. Cigarettes were avidly sought by servicemen, and children equally avidly saved up to purchase them as gifts. (Western Times, 1.9.16)

Exeter's Victoria Hall often had many seats reserved for wounded men by the proprietors and other well-wishers, or purchased through the Comforts Fund. In just one outing, 400 wounded men were taken to the Theatre Royal in convoys of volunteers' cars to see the delectably named farce *A Little Bit of Fluff* and afterwards were given tea and gifts of chocolates and cigarettes. And in preparation for Christmas in Exeter 1915 and 1916, Miss Buller asked for and duly received gifts of tinned and potted meat, chocolates, sweets, cakes, jam, pickles, socks, scarves, cardigans, gloves, pipes, cigarettes, slippers, mufflers, pens, books, mouth organs – and decorations.

During the first twelve months of the war, the Exeter hospitals received 3,500 patients from France and the Dardanelles together with some sick troops from the local barracks; a total of 484 major and 366 minor operations were performed. Ruth Whitaker, the daughter of the rector of Broadclyst, was a VAD trainee nurse in Number 1 Hospital when the first casualties arrived. She and a colleague were ordered to take a bedpan to an amputee. In her memoirs she wrote:

The walk down the ward was hideously short. When we reached the bed the condition of the amputated leg was appallingly evident, to more than one sense. I put my arm under his arm-pit, to give the orthodox lift, and the patient groaned. 'Easy, Nurse, my elbow's gone too.' The leg had been blown off, not amputated, and the stump was terribly septic. Next day he was moved into the little single ward, and I was put on to 'special' him.

She recalled that every jarring of the bed hurt him and his father cried when he saw him, but against all expectations he survived. The men's courage, cheerfulness and 'kindness, to each other and to us' amazed her. For her, their humility was epitomised by bandsman Thomas Rendle, who made nothing of the award of his Victoria Cross when it was announced in the ward and continued to sweep the floor in his dressing gown. She comments that he grew ever 'whiter' when he became the centre of attention by Lord and Lady Fortescue, the city's mayor, his colonel, his local parson and squire, and hordes of relatives. She stated, 'He emerged quite unspoilt.'

Later on Ruth Whitaker became a senior VAD nurse at Streatham Hall Hospital for Officers. One day the peace was broken by 'wild, mad shouts and screams' from an officer's room. She hurried, but 'walking, not running, because running is forbidden to a nurse', and found the officer 'trying to climb out of the lower sash of the third floor window. I was in time to clutch his legs. He stopped screaming and we struggled silently.'

She records that he died shortly afterwards in 'a shell-shock hospital' at Plymouth. It is a rare mention of the little understood and officially denied condition.

In 1915, King George V and Queen Mary visited the war hospitals in Exeter, Torquay and Plymouth. Arriving by royal train at St David's station on 9 September, the king and queen were welcomed by Lord and Lady Fortescue and Mr and Mrs Owen, the mayor and mayoress. They drove through cheering crowds to the High Street, then through Broadgate, past the front of the cathedral to South Street, where 'great crowds from the West Quarter' had gathered, and then on to Magdalen Street and

V.C. FOR AN EXONIAN.

GALLANT RESCUE OF AN OFFICER UNDER FIRE.

The 28th Victoria Cross awarded in the present war has been won by Bandsman Thomas Edward Rendle, 1st Battalion Duke of Cornwall's Light Infantry.

It was near Wulverghem on November 20th that Rendle won the coveted Cross. He was acting in the regimental ambulance when shells from German howitzers blew in a trench at several places. In one isolated section Lieutenant Colebrook was lying with a wound in the thigh which severed the artery. Lieutenant Wingate (whose home is at Cullompton) crawled to him, but decided that it would be impossible to get him back into safety until dark. When further shells pitched close by, how-

ever, Bandsman Rendle undertook the desperate task of conveying the wounded officer back, carrying him on his own back while he wormed his way over the exposed ground on his stomach. After applying a tourniquet to the wound he had to traverse five great shell-holes, and as he emerged from each the German sharpshooters 200 yards away took pot-shots at his head. By dint of scraping at the earth, however, he managed to create some degree of cover, and all three got back to the main trench without incident.

Bandsman Thomas Rendle VC.
(Trewman's Flying Post, 16.1.15)

BRAVERY AWARDS
The foremost award for all ranks was the Victoria Cross (VC).
Second, for officers only, was the Distinguished Service Order (DSO). For junior naval, army and, after April 1918, RAF officers there were, respectively, the Distinguished Service Cross (DSC), Military Cross (MC) instituted in December 1914, the Distinguished Flying Cross (DFC) and Air Force Cross (AFC). For other ranks (corresponding to the officers' awards) there were, second, the Distinguished Conduct Medal (DCM), and then the Distinguished Service Medal (DSM), Military Medal (MM), Distinguished Flying Medal (DFM) and Air Force Medal (AFM).

Number 1 Hospital. The king or queen spoke to each patient. In the evening, local donations enabled the VAD to entertain the royal party at Victoria Hall together with 900 wounded men from the city and its surrounds. The king was gracious in his tributes to the men and to the hospital staff, and picked out Georgiana Buller for especial thanks. In March 1918, the Prince of Wales (the future Edward VIII) paid a fleeting visit to the city on his way to the Duchy of Cornwall estates around Dartmoor. He, too, met Geogiana Buller and inspected the fifty wounded men with her who formed a guard of honour at St David's station.

A few copies of *Tittle-Tattle* survive, a bittersweet magazine written and produced by patients and staff at Number 1 Hospital from 1916 onwards. Number 5 Hospital had a similar magazine, and again a few survive.

The Germans were regularly mocked in verse or cartoons. A doctor contributed:

> There was a German of Kult'ya
> Who felt it a joy to insult ya
> But we put some cold steel
> In a place he could feel
> And left the results for the Vultya.

Men failing to enlist were scorned. One verse of a soldier's poem said:

> Lads how can you sleep in your beds at night
> When you dream of your pals in their fight for the right
> I think it's a shame for you to be walking about
> For you should be put on the boat and sent straight out.

King George V and Queen Mary visit Exeter (their first public use of a motor car). (Devon and Exeter Gazette, 9.9.15)

Nurse Braithwaite served at Number 5 Hospital, and kept an autograph book whose poignant entries reveal her patients' ability to express their feelings in a variety of engaging ways. The pages reveal a sensitive awareness of human relationships, wry humour at hospital regulations and food – especially the alleged overuse of rhubarb – and gratitude for the personal care. Overall, there is more than a hint that for once in their lives the men felt they were being treated as special. There is also an acceptance that the war was a just one, combined with seething anger at conscientious objectors.

One anonymous nurse in Exeter recorded her duties in the *Maynard School Magazine* for 1915. Day duty started at 8.00 a.m. and lasted well over 12 hours and was an endless round of sweeping, dusting and polishing, accompanying the doctors' ward rounds, preparing dressings, administering medicines, serving meals, making beds, washing bandages and, finally, getting patients ready for the night. If all the tasks were completed she left between 9.00 p.m. and 9.30 p.m. Night duty could be particularly distressing when it was punctuated by patients moaning in pain, twisting and turning in nightmares or angrily restless because they could not fall sleep.

The work of the Exeter war hospitals went on under great strain. After the war, the Devon Red Cross and VAD published

 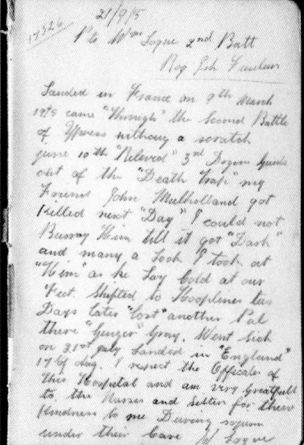 

Nurse Georgina Blathwayt's Common Book – a soldier's drawing of a VAD nurse, possibly Nurse Blathwayt; a soldier's record of service and comments; a soldier's view of conscientious objectors. (Devon Heritage Centre)

The Little V.A.D.'s

Ten little V.A.D.'s thought the soup looked fine,
One brave girl tried it and then there were nine.
Nine little V.A.D.'s came in very late,
One got her head snapped off, then there were eight,
Eight little V.A.D.'s desired a taste of Heaven,
But their billets didn't suit them, so then there were **seven**.
Seven little V.A.D.'s ate some cakes like bricks,
The M.O. went and killed one, then there were six.
Six little V.A.D.'s went out for a drive,
The steering gear was faulty, there came back only **five**.
Five little V.A.D.'s feeling very sore,
Had to be inoculated, then there were four.
Four little V.A.D.'s went out on a spree,
Headquarters got to hear of it, then there were three.
Three little V.A.D.'s had no work to do,
One asked for a transfer and then there were two.
Two little V.A.D.'s heard the war was done.
One died of ecstacy and then there was one.
One little V.A.D. tried to catch a tram,
Caught her foot and stumbled—and you should have heard
         what she said !

Poem 'The Little VADs', from Number 5 Hospital's magazine. (Devon Heritage Centre) a detailed account of their joint wartime activities, and with justification felt satisfied with the immense efforts of over 2,000 Red Cross and VAD staff and many more thousands of helpers and fund raisers. It recorded that 45,475 patients had been admitted to the various hospitals across Devon, but added that these figures only included 'Exeter VA Hospitals prior to their transfer to War Office control'. This refers to the sudden decision of Sir Alfred Keogh, Director General of the Army Medical Service, in late 1915 to place all the Exeter war hospitals

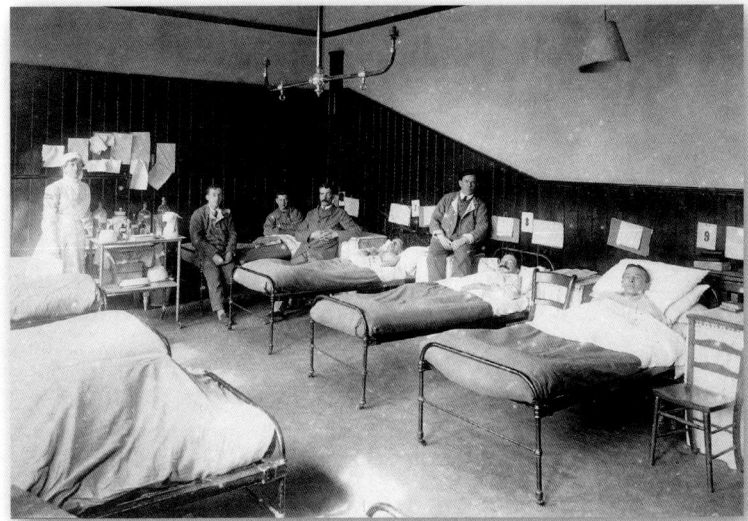

A ward in Number 2 Hospital. (Devon Heritage Centre)

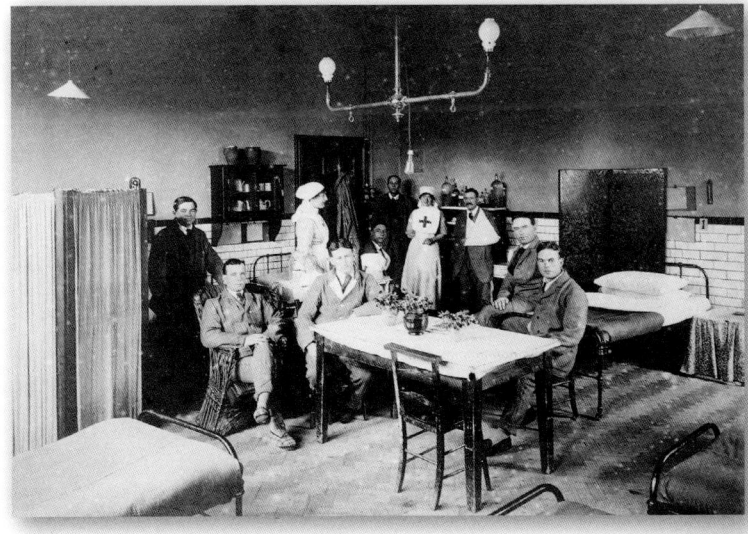

Another ward in Number 2 Hospital. (Devon Heritage Centre)

**DAME GEORGIANA BULLER
(1884–1953)**
Born near Crediton, Georgiana
Buller became the only female
administrator of a major wartime
military hospital complex, for
which she was awarded the
Royal Red Cross First Class and
DBE. Her energy, determination
and renown were instrumental
in founding Princess Elizabeth
Orthopaedic Hospital in 1927
and St Loye's Training Centre
for Cripples in 1937, both in
Exeter, and Queen Elizabeth's
Training College for Cripples
in Leatherhead. She also
established the influential British
Council for Rehabilitation.

under direct military control and, even more controversially, place Georgiana Buller, the daughter of his old friend General Sir Redvers Buller, in supreme command.

This dramatic, and indeed unique, appointment caused considerable resentment. For the remainder of the war the friction between Major Davis, the VAD director, and his erstwhile deputy, Miss Buller, was intense, and Lord Fortescue was often called upon to calm things down. Indeed his memoirs suggest that the friction between Davis, whom he described as 'methodical and businesslike, but a little slow and precise', and Buller, whom he saw as capable but obstinate and aspiring 'to the role of Florence Nightingale' had started the moment the city's war hospitals were set up. Possibly Sir Alfred Keogh thought separation would resolve the problem, but instead several Exeter doctors resigned their war hospital posts, feeling it frustrating and humiliating to work under a young and unqualified but supremely self-confident female civilian. In a serious incident in 1917, only kept secret by DORA, the whole of the VAD senior staff, including Major Davis, were only just prevented from resigning in exasperation at what they believed to be the constant interference, excessive inspections and carping criticisms of Southern Command's officers. It was an unhappy separation of administrative, medical and military responsibilities that came close to doing serious harm to a vital part of the war effort.

On 25 September 1914, a group of women led by Lady Fortescue and Mrs Kendall King, the mayoress, created the Exeter Committee for the Relief of War Refugees. Miss Clara Andrew, who had been a prime mover in collecting clothing to send to Belgium soon after it was invaded, became the honorary secretary. In early October the city became the first provincial centre to receive Belgian refugees. The *Express & Echo* waxed eloquently:

Homeless, yes, but not without a house where they will be warmly welcomed; destitute, perhaps, but not without friends who count it a joy and privilege to do something for those who have done so much for us, but for whose gallantry it is possible we might now all be in arms to repel the invader from our shores.

The refugees arrived by train from London at any time of the day or night; the wartime schedules were unreliable and sometimes trains were misdirected – either to Exeter or somewhere else instead. Usually the refugees numbered around 100, but occasionally the welcoming parties and drivers were almost overwhelmed by as many as 250 tired, dirty and confused Belgian children, parents and grandparents gathering on the platform. On at least two occasions the already homeless refugees were survivors of transport ships torpedoed in the English Channel. Their bewilderment must have become even greater when the mayor, sheriff or town clerk of Exeter embarked upon his welcoming speech.

Miss Andrew and her volunteers used a donated house in Southernhay as their headquarters and were very successful in raising substantial sums of money, gathering vast quantities of new and second-hand clothing, requesting free rooms in houses, hotels, halls and hostels and securing the voluntary services of dozens of drivers and vehicles whenever they were needed. Indeed, support for the refugee campaign was so substantial that no salaried officer or worker was ever employed in Exeter and most of the government's grant was returned to the Treasury after the war.

Exeter became the distribution centre for the whole county as a swiftly extending circle of towns and villages created subsidiary committees to renovate and equip cheaply rented or freely donated houses for Belgian families dispatched from Exeter. Schools, church groups, seaside hotels and local clubs and societies all rallied round to help, and numerous newspaper reports and school logbooks record the pride communities took in looking after 'their' Belgians. Even in the depressing wartime winter of 1916, Barnfield Hall was lavishly decorated with lights, tinsel and a tree at Christmas, and 200 refugees were given tea, presents and a parcel of extra clothing. Exeter also put on special English classes. Some Belgian children attended local Devon schools, although others went to temporary schools set up by Belgian priests.

Helping Belgium was a popular and indeed a fashionable thing to do in the early stages of the war. One of the most notable occasions was the bazaar held in the Bishop's Palace in June 1915 on behalf of wounded Belgian soldiers in the south of France. It was opened by Princess Clementine of Belgium, the cousin of King Albert, who arrived on the royal train to the specially deco-rated city and a Guildhall reception, before being escorted to the bazaar where stalls were run by Lady Clinton, Lady Poltimore, Lady Caroline Courtenay, and several Devon mayoresses. Not surpris-ingly the proceeds and accompanying donations soared to £1,271.

By February 1915, 8,000 refugees had passed through Exeter and been resettled. After then the flow subsided. However, by then some sharp differences of opinion, and perhaps personality clashes, led to Lord Fortescue (with the support of the Central War Refugees Committee in London) creating a new Devon War Refugees Committee, which later became the Devon & Cornwall Committee. For almost a year the Exeter Committee remained independent, although it transferred some of its workers and facilities to the new county committee. Surviving letters and Lord Fortescue's memoirs reveal a sad and rather bruising time, during which Miss Andrew's ad hoc but basically fully functioning arrangements were replaced by something more administratively clear-cut and officially accountable, and she was unwillingly marginalised. To Lord Fortescue's obvious relief, she severed all connection late in 1916. She was replaced as secretary by the more socially elevated Miss Bannatyne, daughter of the owner of the Haldon Estate, assisted by Miss Harrison, daughter of General Sir Richard Harrison, a veteran of wars in the Crimea, China and South Africa and now honorary colonel of several Devon-based army units. In 1917, though, the capable Miss Andrew went on to found the National Child Adoption Agency, and in 1926 she was instrumental in securing the successful passage of the Adoption of Children Act.

Lord Fortescue did not approve of the behaviour of many the refugees, although his speeches to them oozed admiration of their country's valour. In June 1915, the city's chief constable bitterly complained of the repeated 'needless trouble' they caused, especially in wilfully evading the order to report any travel arrangements and changes of address as DORA required. And as early as November 1914, a local article appeared cautioning against the general tendency to 'spoil them'. Almost inevitably, conflicts arose within Belgian communities, and between Belgian and British families, occasionally leading to court cases and fines. No doubt cultural differences, social disparities, language barriers and maybe more than a touch of British insularity played their part. After the war it took until the summer of 1919 for all the refugees to be repatriated, and then Fortescue wrote, '… the office finally closed to the great relief of all connected with it, for the refugees were not a nice lot; they were exacting and tiresome, and a proportion of them were criminal and immoral.' Even the final report of the Devon & Cornwall Committee expressed surprise at the consistent generosity of local people as 'the Refugees were not selected specimens; indeed, sometimes they were not very desirable visitors, and more often than not they were persons with a different standard of living and observance to those who housed them'. In 1918, Miss Andrew was honoured by Belgium with the *Medaille de la Reine Elisabeth* alongside Miss Bannatyne and several district organisers. Miss Bannatyne, however, also received an MBE.

On 10 August 1914, the Mayoress of Exeter, Mrs Kendall King, established the 'Guildhall Depot', which co-ordinated several of the city's charitable collections. Within a couple of weeks it had boxed and dispatched three 'large cases of comforts' including pipes, tobacco, cigarettes, Vaseline, boracic powder, postcards, handkerchiefs and sweets to the 1st Devons in Flanders, and created numerous bales of assorted clothing for local Territorial battalions and for the Red Cross Central Depot in London. In addition 550 extra blankets had been given to the local barracks and locally knitted 'dark blue woollen scarves, mittens and helmets' sent to the elderly cruiser HMS *Devonshire* on patrol in the North Sea.

Towards the end of 1914 the new mayoress, Mrs Owen, took over leadership of the Depot. That Christmas, 2,200 boxes of tobacco and sweets were sent to men in the Devons on the Western Front. The Depot's well-supported Hospitality Fund was regularly providing free refreshments for troops when their trains pulled into St David's station. So appreciative was the War Office that Lord Kitchener ordered news of the time of arrival of the troop trains, normally a closely guarded secret, to be sent by telegram to the mayoress. A total of 11,564 packed meals – each one comprising a milk loaf, butter, ham, an orange, a piece of cake, a packet of cigarettes and enough tea to fill the soldier's water bottle – had been given away by the end of 1914. The demand was relentless. On two days in March 1915, 2,100 packs were handed out at Queen Street station.

Numerous letters reaching the Depot from individual soldiers and company commanders showed how much both the refreshments and the thoughtfulness of the act were appreciated. In May 1915, the father of a young trooper wrote, 'As they had left camp at 11 on the previous evening, you may know how welcome the refreshments were to them.' In 1916, an officer of the Army Service Corps highlighted his men's long and tedious train journey through the night, the many hours without a meal and then the sudden and immensely cheering appearance of the mayoress' refreshment party. An Exonian in the Grenadier Guards was one of many who wrote about his pride at hearing men from other units praise 'the generosity they met with from the Mayoress of our old City and her band of helpers'.

By January 1916, well over half a million packed meals had been given away, but a combination of the mounting costs and the mounting number of trains forced the Depot to reduce the refreshments to a large bun and tea – at 2.5d rather than 6d a head.

In a special ceremony in May 1918, contingents of Australian, New Zealand and South African troops accompanied by their bands marched through the decorated streets of

Miss Andrew's Medaille de la Reine Elisabeth. *(Topsham Museum)*

Mr and Mrs Owen (front row, fourth and fifth from left) and other volunteers at St David's station. (Devon and Exeter Institution)

Exeter to Northernhay Gardens, where senior officers from the Dominions formally thanked the Mayoress of Exeter's Depot for the refreshments provided for their troops at the railway stations. Each country's flag was presented to the city to be hung in the Guildhall. The Canadian flag followed in due course.

The same appreciation was shown towards the parcels reaching the men at sea or abroad. In April 1915, a letter from the West Country crew of HMS *Gossamer*, an elderly torpedo gunboat, said, 'You may be assured that the articles are very welcome, and full use can and will be made of them during the cold days and nights which are experienced up here.' In November 1916, an officer of the Devons wrote that the 'magnificent bale of socks' was 'a tremendous boon' in keeping clean, comfortable and warm. Another unit particularly welcomed the gramophone and records, and a third rejoiced at the relaxation and enjoyment provided by the footballs and accompanying shorts and 'jersies'. Another Exonian wrote, 'It was Sunday when we received your parcel, and we had a jolly good tea that day which reminded us of times at home.' Elsewhere one soldier particularly welcomed the cocoa, and yet another the bars of chocolate to chew or watch melt into a drink. There were many similar letters.

The Guildhall Depot never ceased expanding and spilled over into premises in Pancras Lane. In April 1915, female volunteers in the city were set to work following detailed patterns for the construction of 8,000 gas-mask pads from medicated cotton wool, stockinette, worsted cloth and thick cotton elastic. In October 1915, under the auspices of Queen Mary's Fund, another 'influential committee of ladies' headed by Mrs Owen was formed to encourage more women in the city to spend as much time as they could spare at the Depot 'making surgical bandages and all kinds of hospital necessaries' such as swabs, splints, slings, pillowcases, bed shirts and sphagnum moss bags for local and national use. By the end of 1916 there were 430 helpers on roll, with sixty or so attending each day.

Starting in 1915, parcels were sent to the Devons who were prisoners of war in Germany, and then to those enduring Turkish camps after being captured in Gallipoli or at Kut in Mesopotamia. Strict regulations governed the labels, packaging and content that had to be confined to toiletries (tooth, hair and shaving brushes, toothpaste and soap) and sweets and games, mittens and mufflers and webbing braces and belts. Most of those sent to Germany arrived safely, but far fewer reached Turkish prisons. After news filtered through about the harsh treatment of Turkish prisoners, the Depot started to send money orders so men could try to buy better treatment from their guards. In November 1918, 700 Devon Regiment men were prisoners, most of them as a result of 'misfortunes in the German offensive' over the past year. Nearly 15,000 parcels were sent out that year alone, and overall 22,341 parcels were dispatched to Germany and 804 to Turkey.

Mrs Owen and other volunteers at the Mayoress of Exeter's Depot. (Devon Heritage Centre)

As the war progressed, Lord Fortescue, Mr (later Sir) James Owen, the city council and several Depot committee members became heavily involved in working through the War Office and Red Cross to find out as much as possible about the fate of missing and captured men on behalf of their deeply worried families.

There were endless street collections, with women and convalescing soldiers waving tins and selling flags and badges. 'Our Day' was linked to Trafalgar Day each October and traditionally raised funds for the British Red Cross and local hospitals. In Exeter the 'Our Day' collections in schools and on the streets raised £358 in 1915, £248 in 1916 and £302 in 1917. Typically, in just the second half of 1917 there was Alexandria Rose Day in June on behalf of the civilian hospitals, in July a flag day for the French Red Cross and a Silent Tribute Day for Lord Roberts Memorial Workshop for Disabled Soldiers & Sailors, and in August a massive rummage sale for the War Hospitals' Comforts Fund. In September there was a Roumanian Red Cross Day, in October 'Our Day', in November a collection for King George's Fund for Sailors and in December Exeter's YMCA Hut Week raised £3,000 through street collections, a concert and several sales of work. Scattered throughout the war years were additional collections, such as those for Russian hospitals, the Serbian and Italian Red Cross, as well as Pansy Day for prisoners of war and Butterfly Day for the RSPCA.

Finally, in early 1918, a large painted barometer appeared outside the Guildhall. Regularly updated, it showed how much Exeter's citizens and businesses were investing in the intensively promoted national War Bonds campaign that neatly combined appeals to patriotism with guaranteed interest rates. Based upon its population and rateable value, Exeter's target was a massive £150,000. The publicity posters exclaimed that this was the cost of a destroyer and a 'big squadron of aeroplanes'. In the end, Exeter's citizens and firms invested £254,861 and most other Devon towns also exceeded their targets.

Notices.

EXETER.

Under the auspices of the Mayor and Corporation, by request of the Lord Mayor of London to all Mayors in England.

A

FRENCH RED CROSS DAY

WILL BE HELD

WEDNESDAY, JULY 14th.

STREET SALE OF FLAGS by Young Ladies.

DECORATED TRAMS.

A LANTERN PROCESSION by Exeter Boy Scouts, headed by their Bands.

FETE CHAMPETRE IN THE ROUGEMONT GROUNDS.

COMEDIES FRANCAISES (in French).

Pastoral Dances by Miss Couldridge's Pupils.

CONCERTS by Entente Concert Party.

CONCERTS by Isca Glee Singers.

Plain Teas, 6d. With fruit, 9d. Admission: 2.30 to 6 o'clock, 1s. Afterwards, 6d.

Gifts of Cakes, Cream, Butter, Fruit, &c., will be thankfully received. Postcards of promises to the Hon. Secretary, Mrs. Pastfield, 7, Victoria-terrace, Exeter. Gifts to Mrs. Garnsworthy, Rougemont House, on morning of Fête.

French Red Cross Day publicity notice. (Trewman's Flying Post, 10.7.15)

WOMEN AND
THE WAR

Wartime propaganda heaped praise on women's contribution to the war effort as workers in fields, factories and hospitals. By 1918, some 750,000 were in jobs formerly held by men, 350,000 in jobs created by the war economy and a further 240,000 in agriculture. It has been assumed that these experiences gave women a newfound independence and self-confidence that dramatically separated them from their pre-war 'sisters' – but this conclusion is too simplistic.

There was a backlash against women who tried to hold on to their wartime jobs after the war, especially when the economy suffered a severe downturn in the early 1920s, and women as well as men criticised female workers for stopping family men earning a living wage. Indeed an Act of Parliament forced women out of manufacturing industries. Possibly, though, many women were happy to stop working if patriotism rather than the need to earn money had caused them to accept employment. There is little evidence that middle-class women stayed working, or that many upper-class women ever strayed beyond charity work and helping in the family mansion when it became a hospital. The exceptions received much publicity – largely because they were the exceptions. And right through the war, and long afterwards, sweated labour and poor wages remained common in most areas of female employment, alongside dubious safety practices and authoritarian working regimes.

For many working-class women, paid employment as domestic servants or factory workers was as familiar a feature of their lives as being wives and mothers running the home. Earning money did not always cease on marriage, as was expected in 'white-collar' occupations such as schoolteachers and clerks. The only difference the war made to many female workers was the greater danger of losing their menfolk.

However, women workers did become far more visible to the general public, notably, for example, on railway stations, buses and trams. Their abilities were generally well regarded and they were widely, if temporarily, accepted. Letters and diaries reveal women's pride in their wartime roles. Many had had to leave home to find employment and they learned to make their own way in the world – and take advantage of new opportunities. They set a bold example, and, despite all the post-war difficulties, perhaps this was their long-lasting achievement.

4

NEWS FROM THE FRONT

As early as 19 September 1914, the *Flying Post* rightly called the conflict the 'World's Greatest War'. But, in April 1915, it was wrong to assert 'the war has not yet touched the people of Exeter very much'.

Well before the end of 1914, long lists of volunteers had appeared in that same newspaper. Men from the city were serving in a wide variety of units. The third Exeter roll of honour published in October 1914 named those serving not only in the 1st, 3rd, 4th, 7th and 8th battalions of the Devon Regiment but also the Rifle Brigade, the Royal Field Artillery, 1st Dragoon Guards, Royal Engineers, Northumberland Fusiliers, Duke of Cornwall's Light Infantry, Royal Army Medical Corps, Royal Marines, the battleships HMS *Centurion, Illustrious* and *Orion*, and the cruisers HMS *Bellona, Roxburgh* and *Theseus*. And men from many other towns and counties, especially in the Midlands, found themselves in the Devons.

At least eight of the Devons battalions were raised in Exeter and probably a significant proportion of city men were to be found in them. The stories of their travels and battles featured regularly in the newspapers and, as we have seen, the Mayoress of Exeter's Depot focused much of its attention on this widely scattered regiment whose battalions served in France, Italy, India, Gallipoli, Egypt and Mesopotamia, as well as England.

Initially the stories were largely travelogues, describing the men's journeys away from Exeter and Devon. As we have seen, when war was declared the city cheered the tired and hungry

Devon and Cornish battalions as they passed through the streets to the station after decamping on Woodbury Common. On 29 August 1914, readers could follow the route of B Company Cyclists from the 7th Devons as they wound their way peacefully from Exeter to Kingsbridge and then were called to Totnes where they boarded a train for 22 hours of tedious travel to a secret northern destination – actually Seaton Carew, near Hartlepool. Here they underwent intensive training, including frightening night patrols with glaring searchlights probing the sky, against a background of constant invasion rumours and alarms.

The 4th, 5th and 6th Territorial battalions were dispatched to India and accounts of their voyages in the autumn of 1914 describe, frequently with awe, the stately convoy guarded by mighty warships as it ploughed across the Bay of Biscay and then passed the celebrated Rock of Gibraltar looming above the mist. The men wrote about how they enjoyed the gloriously cool blood-red sunsets of the Mediterranean, laughed at the clamour of small bobbing boats at Suez with their owners offering oranges, figs, postcards and tobacco for sale, and watched the flying-fish displays in the Arabian Sea. And then they had to endure the growing and almost unbearable heat of the tropics, and get used to the pungent smells of spice, dirt and dung in Bombay. Writing home to Exeter, Corporal F. W. Lias of the 4th Devons described the strange sights on his lengthy railway journey across India – especially the numerous garish temples and statues of gods, usually in animal form, and the striking gorges and waterfalls along a route winding high up some unknown mountains. Eventually the battalion ended up at Ferozepore in the Punjab, the centre of a discontented region that had caused the British trouble since the Indian Mutiny of 1857. Few men liked the flat, dry and dusty landscape surrounding the camp.

INDIA IN THE FIRST WORLD WAR
Fears of Indian nationalist uprisings in 1914 were unfounded. India rallied to the Allied cause and 800,000 Indian troops fought on the Western Front, in Gallipoli and Africa, with 1.5 million volunteering to fight. A total of 47,746 were recorded as killed or missing, and 65,000 wounded. Afghanistan's Amir Habibullah Khan maintained his friendship with Great Britain, despite German entreaties, until his murder in February 1919 allowed a hostile son to launch an ill-fated invasion of India.

The 1st Battalion took part in the Battle of the River Aisne in September 1914. There was a strenuous march towards the battle with the sound of guns getting louder. The men spent the night of 14–15 September in torrential rain, and then were ordered into poorly sited and inadequately constructed trenches, where a great spur of German trenches could cover them with enfilading fire. They endured constant shelling and sniping and incurred 100 casualties, but they made substantial improvements to the trenches and the lines of communication before moving back for rest and recuperation. Private Fred Dymond of Preston Street was invalided home after his neck was hit by a piece of shrapnel. He remembered how the Germans gauged the range by information signalled back by their aircraft, and how his comrades tried desperately hard to dig themselves in. He liked the French – 'He gabbles on; you don't understand, but you laugh loudly, and say in a sort of way, "Yes. Yes."' His family was luckier than that of Mrs Kilgannon of Cotton Buildings with four children aged between nineteen months and seven years, who were left without a husband or father. Drummer Kilgannon had died of his wounds on 20 September, but for some reason his wife had not been told of his injury and news of his death took three weeks to arrive home.

Writing from Flanders that November, Lt Jerman tried to convey what it was like to experience a bombardment while he was driving through a shattered town. The heavy vibrations made the tiles, walls and even the pavement shake and the arrival of heavy shells were presaged by a 'deadly hum' but where they were going to land no one knew. The 'flash, bang and smoke' wrecked and distorted everything in sight, and the tinkling of falling glass was 'weird' and constant. He found he was skidding into the front of a house and some time later he noticed a piece of shrapnel had made holes in the back and roof of the car. His family back in Exeter was spared no detail.

On a couple of strange days things were a little different in some parts of the front line. In early January 1915, Pte Leslie Jenks' family received a letter saying, 'I was up in the trenches for Christmas, but honestly I enjoyed my Christmas very much and wouldn't have missed the experience for any amount of money.

As regards puddings, we ate so much that we looked like them.'
Then he said:

> This was the extraordinary part of our Christmas. By means of shouting across to each other's trenches we came to a mutual agreement that we would not fire during the Christmas, so on Christmas Eve night we were walking about between the lines, and on Christmas Day we actually played football. I went over myself to the Germans and obtained a few signatures, also cigars and cigarettes from them – a very decent lot of fellows. The weather for Christmas was very dry and cold, with a hard frost.

Then he added, '[name omitted] was hit the day before Christmas Eve. The bullet entered his cheek and came out at the back of his head.'

Other Christmases were celebrated as well as the circumstances allowed, but there seems to have been no more fraternisation with the enemy. A *Western Times* reporter serving in the Devons described Christmas Day 1917 on the Western Front. The men attended divine service and the singing was 'bright and hearty'. Rolls of white paper were allowed as tablecloths and the men used knives and forks, not the usual fingers and jackknife. Sergeants and corporals carved and served roast beef and pork with apple sauce, boiled potatoes and turnips, which replaced the usual bully beef and stew. Christmas pudding and drinks followed, and gifts were opened 'from the Fairy God-Mother of the Devon Regiment, the Mayoress of Exeter, and also Mrs Chapple of Starcross'. The men had performed a concert on Christmas Eve and a football match was played on Christmas Day afternoon. Light snow fell afterwards.

THE 1914 CHRISTMAS TRUCE
About 100,000 soldiers are estimated to have taken part in this unofficial event. It started in the German trenches around Ypres, with carols and greetings wafting across to the British lines. Cautiously men peered, then clambered, over the parapets to meet, talk, exchange gifts, sing carols and play games with each other in No Man's Land. Some men, especially senior generals, disapproved and initially the news was censored in Germany and Great Britain. The following year, bombardments and attacks were ordered over Christmas, and only unsupported rumours existed of further truces.

Overall the winter in the still-primitive trenches was uncomfortable as well as dangerous and hatred of the enemy became a common factor in letters home. In February 1915, Pte F. J. Parker, a city fireman, now in the Coldstream Guards, wrote home that, 'We have been put to a very severe test during the winter, often standing up to our knees in mud and water for hours at a time before being relieved, and then having nowhere to get ourselves dry.' He spoke of men enraged by German atrocities, and of a colleague in particular, 'who, having his rifle put out of action, went for them with his fists. I am afraid, however, that he won't have the chance again, as I heard he received several bayonet wounds.' Private S. W. Wood of Clifton Street was among the 2nd Devons who cleared a German trench at Neuve Chapelle and his letter home, like many others describing personal experiences, spared no details of the bombs he threw into it, the dazed Germans they captured and the trench 'running with blood' from the dead and injured men.

Private C. Kerslake wrote to his brother in Old Tiverton Road from France, in August 1915, about the 'terrible bombardments, attacks and counter attacks, shells, bombs, fire, everything one can think of that is destructive to life and limb'. His hatred of the Germans was acute, especially when two comrades were 'blinded by vitriol by these monsters'. Like many men crawling desperately through the mud, noise and blood, he looked up at the fighter planes engaged in acrobatic duels over the lines and rejoiced at British triumphs. 'Talk about a hawk and a pigeon,' he gloated. 'The swoop down, the setting fire to the Hun aeroplane, which dropped like a ball of fire, the aviator jumping out in mid-air, while the observer stuck to the burning plane and fell into the lines of the Cornwalls.' In January 1916, 2nd-Lt Charles Tudor-Jones was not so lucky. Flying as observer for Lt Alan Hobbs, both men were killed when their Morane 'parasol' was engaged and shot down by the German ace Max Immelmann. Before the war, Tudor-Jones had been articled to an Exeter solicitor, and in common with many airmen, he was formerly an infantryman – in his case a captain in the 7th Devon Cyclists Battalion.

Getting wounded men to safety was often hazardous. In March 1915, Lance Corporal H. R. Vincent from St Thomas, serving in the Royal Army Medical Corps, wrote of the nightly search parties on the Western Front. Often under German fire, the stretcher-bearers heaved or carried wounded men to the motor ambulances that then, without any lights, lurched around the numerous potholes in the rough track to a makeshift hospital in an old school. For many men, he said, the touch of the surgeon's knife was feared more than the battle itself. Dr Herbert Child from Exeter served at Gallipoli during the disastrous Allied Campaign between April 1915 and January 1916 to secure a sea route to Russian Black Sea ports through the Turkish-held Dardanelles Straits. Forewarned by long-winded Allied preparations, the Turks had had time to mass their forces and dig in. Part of his account for *Medical World* was reprinted in chilling detail in the *Flying Post*. On the troopship serving as a hospital, he ran out of medical supplies and was reduced to asking sailors to pick out the oakum in the ship's seams, which was placed on top of rags soaked in turpentine to stop wounds oozing. Splints were made from bayonet cases and any odd bits of wood. Many soldiers had been wounded twice, once in the land battle and again when the ferry boats were targeted by the Turks. Exonians also fought the Turks across vast areas of Mesopotamia, marching through the swamps and deserts between the Euphrates and Tigris, seizing Basra, and fighting the Turks successfully all the way to Kut – only for a humiliating British surrender to occur there in April 1916. Others were stationed in garrisons in Egypt, then a British protectorate but troubled by nationalist unrest that was encouraged by German agents and promises of support.

Exeter also heard from a woman on the Western Front. Elizabeth Shapter, the daughter of Dr Thomas Shapter, was born in Exeter in 1884. Despite – or probably because of – her flamboyant and unconventional lifestyle, not least as an enthusiastic and risk-taking motorcyclist, she attained fame as a courageous nurse in the heart of the desperate fighting around Ypres. Elizabeth – generally known as Elsie – and her friend Mairi Chisholm became Red Cross ambulance drivers taking

*'In the Land of the Pharoahs.' Turkish threats, the Suez Canal and Senussi tribal revolts kept many British troops in Egypt, including some Devons. (*Western Times*, 12.10.17*

In the Land of the Pharoahs.

THE above photograph has been sent home by Pte. A. V. Call (centre), of Summerland-street, who joined the forces about two years ago. All three hail from the "Ever Faithful." Pte. Call is attached to a Lewis gun section, and has been in a good many "mix-ups" with the Turks. In one engagement he had the legs of his gun tripod shot away, and, to use his own words, thought it was a close "Call." Pte. Call, previous to joining up, was a fine exponent of the natatory art, and was Captain of the Exeter Polo Team. His knowledge of swimming stood him in good stead, as he was the means of saving the life of a comrade while bathing in the Suez Canal. He has two other brothers serving, one in India and the other training "somewhere in England."

wounded men from just behind the lines to field hospitals. However, they came to believe that more lives could be saved if wounded men received the quickest possible treatment at the front, not least to allay shock, and, in November 1914, after being spurned by the Red Cross, they set up their own independent dressing station in a cellar at Pervyse, just north of Ypres, and only 100 yards from the trenches. For three and a half years, with battles raging around them, they rescued and treated casualties, often under fire, and then transported them to the base hospital 15 miles away. Their undoubted bravery was recognised with the Belgian Order of Leopold II and, belatedly, the British Military Medal. Socially well connected, they took numerous photographs in order to raise funds in Belgium and Great Britain for medical supplies, and, at one time, for concrete reinforcements to their rickety dressing station. Already married and divorced, although not admitting it, Elsie married a Belgian Roman Catholic airman in January 1916 and became Baroness T'Serclaes, but that marriage failed too. However, it was as the baroness, and ex-pupil of the Maynard School, that she visited Exeter in May 1916 to speak about their work, and to raise funds, at a public meeting in the Barnfield Theatre. Elsie and Mairi's war ended in March 1918 when they were gassed and had to return to England. Their friendship abruptly ended when Mairi learnt of Elsie's marital deception.

The 8th and 9th Devons were at the Battle of Loos where they captured four German 77mm howitzers. The battle had lasted from 25 September until 14 October 1915, and was part of an initially successful but ultimately frustrated attempt by British and French armies to break the German defences in Artois and Champagne. On the first day, the 8th Devons, with the 9th Devons in reserve, charged the enemy trenches. In the withering fire they lost nearly all their officers. Nevertheless, the remnants of the battalion seized the forward trench and then the one behind it. Assaulted by German howitzers but luckily hidden by smoke and noise, the battalion formed two raiding

*Elsie Shapter (left) and Mairi Chisholm at Pervyse. (*Illustrated War News*, 1917)*

On the British Western front: fair Wearers of "Tin Hats."

parties and surprised and overran the guns. They held on despite counterattacks until relieved the following day. By then, only a third of the 8th Devons and half of the 9th remained standing.

Almost certainly referring to the later stages of the battle, although not naming it, Corporal Pidsley wrote home celebrating the British soldiers courage and resolve in attack against 'huge difficulties. The sight was magnificent, and we forgot our own weariness as with moistened eyes we cheered them, their courage and unflinching devotion were so superb.' The corporal rightly admired the achievement of his comrades in arms close by, although understandably he could not appreciate their role in the far more wide-ranging battle. Indeed, it was the equally steadfast opposition of the Germans that thwarted the overall Allied advance.

Two of the captured howitzers were presented to the city on 12 November 1915, which, appropriately perhaps, turned out to be wet and gloomy. Nevertheless, large crowds and the survivors of the two battalions watched the guns hauled by black Royal Field Artillery horses from Queen Street station along South Street, Coombe Street, West Street, Fore Street and the High Street to Northernhay Gardens where, after several speeches eulogising the battalions and honouring the fallen, Lord Fortescue formally handed them over to the mayor and Corporation. Perhaps there was an element of celebration during the event, but all the reports suggest the mood was as sombre as the weather. At least eight non-commissioned officers (NCOs) and men from Devon who fought at the desperate Battle of Loos were awarded the Distinguished Conduct Medal.

On 1 July 1916, the 2nd Battalion took part in an attack on the heavily defended German position in the French village of Pozières. It commenced with an hour's artillery bombardment of the enemy lines, but a few minutes before it ceased the battalion advanced in open order towards the German trenches 100 yards away. At first the opposing fire was not heavy, but when the bombardment lifted a hail of machine-gun fire mowed down the men and very few reached the German lines. Those who did were overcome by the enormous odds and killed. The Germans then began to snipe wounded men and bombard the British trenches with both explosive shells and gas so that communications were severely disrupted. Even when wounded men managed to struggle back to their own trenches, many passageways were blocked by debris. Medical officers crawled to the front line to attend as many wounded men as possible and stretcher-bearers resorted to carrying men on their backs to the Aid Posts, but there were too few bearers. There were barely forty-eight survivors and the exhausted battalion pulled out during the night. Thousands more soldiers, mainly Australian, died that month trying to take and then hold the shattered village.

Late that November, an officer wrote a poignant letter home about the graves of the eleven officers and 149 men from the 2nd Devons:

> They are all buried in the 'Devon Cemetery' in the front line trenches which they left at 7.30 that morning. It is unusually placed at this point, in the right angle crowning the corner of a little wooded bluff – trees all shattered of course, but some undergrowth of thorn and elm still living. There's a valley in front, leading down to a large valley on the right, through which run a road and a railway, and up the hill to the west and south is a gentle slope. It all reminds very much of Dartmoor – easy, gentle slopes – but is rich land, though now foul with thistles.

Two injured men, one from Gallipoli and one from the Western Front, wrote poems while in hospitals in Exeter about their experiences, and their accompanying emotions (see overleaf). The date is August 1916, and possibly the anonymous poem 'Blighty' refers to Pozières. That month, a photograph of eight smiling 'Exeter lads' relaxing at a rest centre behind the lines in Flanders was enough to give the *Western Times* the opportunity to condemn the 'whining pessimists' about the interminable war. By then, though, tens of thousands of Allied troops had been slaughtered in the Battle of the Somme and over 400,000 British soldiers would have been killed, injured, captured or recorded as missing by the time the attacks and counter-attacks petered out in mid-November. One of

THE CHARGE.

Forward they charged with might and main,
To the hill top far away,
With bayonets fixed and not a word,
The Turks around in hundreds slain.

But what a sight when night time came,
Across that sandy plain,
To see the heroes of that fight
Lying there quiet, blood-stained.

Their guns were just like crackers,
And your pals in droves were slain,
But it never broke the hearts of those
Who filled the ranks again.

There's many a broken heart, my friend,
In old England this day,
Who would of you feel mighty proud
If you would join the fray.

So come, buck up, you slackers,
And help your brothers true,
Who have borne the brunt of battle
All for the sake of you.

I speak to you young men at home,
With your comforts in galore,
Just think of those who have died for you,
And come, your revenge to score.

Pte. Panter, 1st Glosters.

"BLIGHTY".

Yes! I've been to fight the Germans
And I've come back home again,
To the dear old land called "Blighty"
Where we soon forget our pain,
What if your leg be punctured by a lump of German shell,
Didn't we strafe the blighters, tho!
Oh! didn't we give them Hell.
---oOo---
Well! and now I lie and think of times
Mid pillows and sheets of white
When we sat with our knees in mud and slime
How we cursed as we gazed at the enemy lines
Oh those square-headed brutes shall pay for their crimes.
"Wait and See."
- -oOo---
Well! the order goes forth and we charge in a row
And we stormed all their trenches, and killed all the foe
For We've scores to pay off for pals that are dead
And Fritz stands no earthly when Tommy sees red,
So it's onward to Glory, for such we were born
But I got to "Blighty" So Happy, What's Your'n?
---oOo---

those from Exeter was Capt. George White from Paris Street, an enthusiastic member of the city's Motor Cycling Club. His father was a city councillor, his mother a prominent helper at the Mayoress of Exeter's Depot, and his young wife was now a widow with a baby son. He had fallen wounded leading his section in a charge, but jumped up and moved on crying out, 'Come on boys! I'll lead you down!' but was then shot through the head. He was just one of thousands of young officers who perished leading their men.

The perils of the war at sea were soon brought home to the city. On 6 August, just a few days after the outbreak of war, the light cruiser HMS *Amphion* was sunk by a mine off the Thames Estuary, probably one laid not long before by the German ship *Konigin Luise* that had been sunk by destroyers accompanying *Amphion*. Two Exeter men survived but one, George Luxton, was among the 150 British sailors who died.

The Battle of Jutland fought between British and German fleets across hundreds of square miles of the misty North Sea on 31 May and 1 June 1916 was a huge national disappointment. Initially confusion reigned, with one local headline proclaiming 'OUR NAVAL VICTORY:

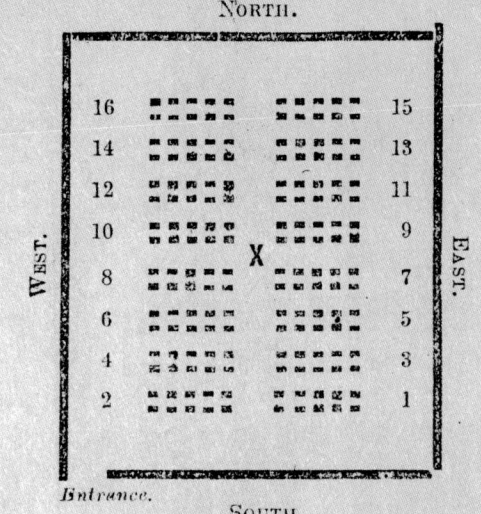

*The map of the graves at Poziéres. (*Trewman's Flying Post, *25.11.16)*

A Tonic for the Depressed.

IT does one's heart good to turn away from the whining pessimists to look at a picture like this. Let who will be glum. Thomas Atkins, Esq., always smiles. This photograph of Exeter lads was sent to us from Flanders with a note thanking the staff of the "Western Times" for a small parcel which was sent out. "The cigarettes," the writer says, "came in very handy. A cigarette is always a chap's best pal out here." The men are (reading from left to right): Standing—Ptes. Warren, Cross and Webber. Sitting—Ptes. Mogridge, Youldon, Corpl. Sutton and Pte. Hewlett. In front, and wearing a monacle, is Pte. Amery.

'A Tonic for the Depressed.' In general, troops served a week or so in forward trenches, a week in support trenches, a week in reserve trenches and then a week in rest centres behind the lines – as pictured here. These men would be returning to the front line shortly. (Western Times, 25.8.16)

Twenty Enemy Vessels Believed to be Sunk' although another soon modestly claimed 'A DRAW' with each side losing fourteen ships. Both were proved wrong as less welcome news trickled through. In the confused and subsequently controversial battle, the Germans lost 3,039 men and eleven ships, but only one was a battlecruiser. The British lost 6,784 men and fourteen vessels: six were capital ships – three battlecruisers and three armoured cruisers. It was far from the expected repeat of Lord Nelson's Trafalgar triumph in 1805, but the German High Seas Fleet never sought another major confrontation with the British Grand Fleet. At least twenty-six men from Exeter or with strong links with it had died. One was Able Seaman John Evans, aged 22, from Garden Square off North Street in Exeter, who was serving on

WE record with regret that Capt. George White, eldest son of the late Mr. Councillor John White, of Paris-street, Exeter, was killed in the British advance on the Somme. He was slightly wounded in the side, but continued at the head of his section, when he received a bullet in the head, which proved fatal. Pte. Russon one of the wounded who arrived at Exeter this week, says after being wounded Captain White jumped up and shouted "Come on boys! I'll lead you down," and was immediately killed. Very great sympathy will be felt with his mother (who is a prominent worker on behalf of the Mayoress's Depot) and his widow, who is left with a baby son.

On the "Indefatigable."

The above four were members of H.M.S. Indefatigable. The one sitting on the left is John Evans, of 10, Garden Square, North-street, Exeter, aged 22 years. This lad's father is also serving his country, and is at present in hospital at Salonika. The one sitting on the right is Alfred Dew, of Queen's Terrace, Dawlish, and is 20 years of age. An elder brother, John Dew, was killed in the charge of the Devons at Loos in September last. Official information of these two having lost their lives has been received.

The death of Captain George White.
(Western Times, 14.7.16)

An Exonian on HMS Indefatigable.
(Western Times, 9.6.16)

HMS *INDEFATIGABLE*

A fast battlecruiser, HMS *Indefatigable* was completed in 1911. She weighed 18,800 tonnes, carried eight 12-inch guns, and had a crew of 800. She served in the Mediterranean and the Dardanelles and then joined Admiral Beatty's 2nd Battlecruiser Squadron. At Jutland, salvoes from the *Von der Tann* caused a magazine to explode and she blew up. There were two survivors.

HMS Indefatigible. *(www.shipspictures.co.uk)*

the battlecruiser HMS *Indefatigable* when it was struck by a full salvo of German shells and immediately blew up. Seamen Jack Kneel and Fred Willey were lost on the armoured cruiser HMS *Defence*, and Commander Harry Pennell and Sub-Lt C.H. Rider, two 'Old Boys' who boarded at Exeter School, were lost on the battlecruiser HMS *Queen Mary*. These ships, too, blew up when hit by heavy salvoes.

Hitting the nation almost as hard was the drowning of Field Marshal Earl Kitchener, the Secretary of State for War, when the ship taking him to Russia was sunk off the Orkneys four days after the Battle of Jutland. Senior politicians and military personnel had become disenchanted with him, but the nation as a whole still revered him as a war leader. All over Exeter, flags were hung at half-mast and on 9 June the cathedral was packed for the memorial service, with city and county dignitaries, army and navy officers, troops from the local barracks and hospitals, VAD nurses, army and navy cadets, and as many other people who could secure a seat. Part of the service included prayers for all those who had died at sea in the war.

Some families had multiple sorrows. Lieutenant Cecil Parsons was killed on 16 July 1916 and his brother, Capt. Maurice Parsons three days later. Just over a year later, Mr Albert Clow of Codrington Street in Newtown was told one son, Pte Henry Clow, had fallen in action on 31 July and his second son, Pte Earnest Clow, had died from wounds he received the previous October. Soon afterwards, Earnest's widow received notification he had been awarded the Military Medal.

On 27 May 1918, the 2nd Devons took part in a desperate and heroic fight at Bois de Buttes on the first day of the third Battle of the Aisne. The previous day the battalion had occupied old trenches and tunnels in a wooded hill just outside La Ville-aux-Bois in an area constantly fought over by the French and Germans in previous years. They were 1,000 yards behind the front line but a German attack quickly overran it and the 2nd Devons suddenly found themselves the only large cohesive force in the way of a massive German advance. Recognising the obstacle the Devons posed, especially to the supply route below the hill, the Germans repeatedly attacked with tanks, infantry and aircraft. Each attack was fought off, but gradually the dwindling battalion was surrounded. With ammunition low, the few dozen survivors undertook a fighting retreat, inevitably losing more men. During the stand, 552 officers and men were killed or captured, but the German advance had been held up long enough for other British and French units to reorganise and halt the German advance a few days later. The achievement and the sacrifice, and France's award of the Croix de Guerre with Palms to the battalion, were blazoned across the local newspapers. An official report of the action was read in all Devon schools.

The citizens of Exeter had been constantly regaled with stories of heroism and death. In some cases photographs accompanied the accounts and reminded readers that local men were scattered across the globe. In July 1916, for example, four Exeter men were featured whose actions in East Africa, at Loos, on the Western Front and in Gallipoli resulted in three Military Crosses and a Distinguished Conduct Medal. The headline was: 'Men Who Add Lustre to Exeter's Name.'

Men Who Add Lustre to Exeter's Name.

THE third Military Cross to come to Exeter during the war has just been awarded to Captain R. S. Townsend, of the Indian Medical Service, fourth son of the late Mr. James Townsend and of Mrs. Townsend, 2, The Crescent, Exeter. He has received this distinction for good service in East Africa, where he has been engaged with the Expeditionary Force since the beginning of operations there. Captain Townsend is No. 1 of the photos above. Another holder of the Military Cross is (2) Lieut. Francis Trott, son of Mr. J. Trott, of the Royal Albert Memorial College. Lieut. Trott won this distinction for gallantry at the battle of Loos last year, he and another officer digging themselves in with their men and holding some guns against a fierce German counter-attack. Both officers were wounded. The other Cross belongs to Lieut. C. E. W. Birkett (3), who when he received it was a Second-Lieutenant of the Somerset Light Infantry, attached to the King's Royal Rifle Corps. He has since been made transport officer and Acting Adjutant in recognition of his services. The only son of Mr. E. W. Birkett, Claremont, Exeter, Lieut. Birkett was, previous to the war, in business at Shepton Mallet. He was wounded at Neuve Chapelle.—The fourth photo is that of Sub-Conductor J. G. Turner, A.O.C., of 11, Ferndale road, St. Thomas, Exeter, who has been awarded the D.C.M. for gallantry in Gallipoli. He has been twice mentioned in despatches. Sub-Conductor Turner is at present in Egypt.

The Men who Add Lustre to Exeter's Name.' (Western Times, 28.7.16)

Late in 1917, two brothers, Capt. and Sgt Jenks, won the Military Cross and Distinguished Conduct Medal respectively for seizing German positions and taking prisoners in two separate incidents. There were many similar stories of courage in the city's newspapers. A blue and white plaque on the wall of a house in Southernhay honours the Revd Theodore Hardy, a Lincolnshire Regiment chaplain, who was born in Barnfield House. The plaque was not placed there until 2006, and his heroism and death received little local attention. However, his remarkable, and repeated, bravery in ministering to and rescuing wounded men under heavy fire on the Western Front led to the awards of the Military Cross, Distinguished Service Order and Victoria Cross. On 18 October 1918, less than a month before the end of the war, he was mortally wounded in the midst of yet another battle.

On several occasions in 1917–19, troops stationed in Exeter gathered in Northernhay Gardens with the mayor, civic and church dignitaries and a large crowd of relatives and well wishers for ceremonies in which a Southern Command general officer presented bravery awards to twenty or so men, mainly from Exeter and south Devon. Sometimes, if the award was posthumous, the man's widow or child would ascend the platform to receive the medal.

The Revd Theodore Bailey Harvey VC DSO MC memorial.
(Tony Ovens)

Erected by Exeter City Council and The Devon Armed Forces Charities 27th June 2006

In Memory of
The Revd Theodore Bayley Hardy
VC DSO MC

Chaplain to the King

Born 20th October 1863
Barnfield House
Died of wounds 18th October 1918
Rouen aged 54

"A Gallant Christian Soldier"
and
"Army Chaplain"

With the gift of hindsight, it is particularly poignant to see the faces and read the deaths of Exeter men who died in the final days of the war. Among them are Gunner John Ewings, Pte Geo. Blackmore, Pte E.G. Hambly, L/Cpl J.C. Upright and L/Cpl Geo. Curtis, all of whom were featured in the *Western Times* on 1 November 1918. The news of other deaths from wounds and disease did not reach homes until after the Armistice, and many families never found out how, or exactly when and where, their menfolk had died.

'Devon Lives Sacrificed on the Altar of Duty.'
(Western Times, 1.11.18)

Devon Lives Sacrificed on the Altar of Duty.

Gunner Ewings.   Pte. Blackmore.   Pte. Hambly.   Lee.-Cpl. Upright.   Lee.-Cpl. Chas. Curtis.

GUNNER JOHN EWINGS, R.F.A., of 16, Cheeke-street, Exeter, has been killed in action in Macedonia. Gunner Ewings, whose mother lives in Porchplace, St. Sidwell's, leaves a widow and five little children, the youngest 5½ years. He was 32 years of age.

PTE GEO. BLACKMORE, M.G.C., son of Mr. and Mrs. Blackmore, of Star-cross, and formerly of Clyst St. Lawrence,

was killed by a shell in France at the age of 18. He went across only about a month ago.

PTE. E.G HAMBLY, Welsh Regiment, of 7, Devonia-terrace, Alphington, who died of wounds on October 26th, 1918, had served over two years in France, and was 28 years of age. Pte. Hambly was a native of Bideford, and a general

favourite at Alphington. He leaves a young widow.

LCE.-CPL. J. C. UPRIGHT, Royal Berks Regt., eldest son of Mr. and Mrs R. C. Upright, Barnfield-road, Exeter, fell in action in France on October 14th. Deceased was only 19 years of age. His lamented death has cut short a life of much promise.

LCE.-CPL GEO. CHARLES CURTIS, Devons, son of Mrs. Curtis, 11, Danes-road, Exeter, was killed in action in France on October 7th. He was 28 years of age, a young man of much promise, and was well-known in the City. At the time of joining the Army, Lce.-Cpl. Curtis was a senior assistant at Eland Bros. High-street.

A Soldier's Life in the Trenches

By November 1914, after a few weeks of fluid fighting to halt the German advance, two continuous lines of trenches from 30–300 metres apart faced each other through villages, farmland and forests and across river valleys and hills, all the way from the Channel coast to Switzerland. The only way each side could advance was by a frontal attack, and if that attack succeeded, the defeated side had to start digging again or fall back into reserve trenches. Trenches of sorts also existed in sandy Palestine, and amidst the rocks and scrub of Gallipoli.

The trenches were not straight but comprised a series of bays at right angles, so that explosions were contained within a short section and an enemy leaping into a trench had a limited field of fire and vision. Short trenches called 'saps' were dug into 'No Man's Land' in front of the trenches, where men watched and listened for signs of enemy activity at night. Some metres behind the front-line trench, and roughly parallel to it, ran one or more support trenches with short connecting trenches. The support trenches had timber-supported 'dugouts' cut into their sides, which provided shelter for troops, signallers and junior officers. Here the soldiers ate and slept, read and wrote letters, tried to keep clean and waited for the next period of duty or enemy attack.

The infantrymen had to learn to avoid the attention of snipers and to miti-
gate the perils of waterlogged, rat-infested and lice-ridden trenches – but
many men were shot, and many more succumbed to fever, frostbite or trench
foot. Duckboards along the bottom of trenches helped offset the perils of
deep water and cloying mud, and the deepest possible latrines helped miti-
gate the stench and health hazards of poor sanitation. Fresh water was in
short supply. In short, men lived in squalor with the added danger of enemy
bullets, shells and bayonets.

Several rows of huge coils of barbed wire stretched out in front of the
trenches. Major attacks on enemy trenches were heralded by heavy artillery
barrages targeting the barbed wire entanglements as much as the trenches,
but bitter experience showed that sufficient wire, defenders and machine
guns usually survived to decimate the men charging across No Man's Land.

5

WHILE YOU WERE AWAY

The husbands, brothers, relatives and friends of many families might have been away in the armed forces, but every day those left behind in the city were reminded of the bitter conflict around the world. Men in a wide variety of uniforms were everywhere and held a wide variety of feelings about past battles, or the battles they might face. Well-guarded trains carrying hundreds of German prisoners of war paused briefly at the city's Queen Street station on their way to camps at Plymouth. 'There was something strangely silent' about these moments, said the *Flying Post* in autumn 1914.

By February 1915, city retailers had noticed significant changes in wholesale supplies and in customers' demands. Business was 'not quite as usual' in tailoring, where the sale of women's more costly outfits, especially evening wear, had fallen away, but the demand for officer's well-tailored military clothing had soared. Many shops reported that rail deliveries from British suppliers were now slow and uncertain, and undoubtedly the North Sea and English Channel were increasingly perilous for shipping. Imported raw flax and linen goods had soared 150% in price as exports from Belgium and Russia dried up, and the absence of German dyes had severely limited the colours of cotton goods. No one wanted eau de cologne, and French or even English perfumes were much preferred. Shopkeepers reported that pharmaceuticals, musical instruments, binoculars and cameras were in short supply as most had come from Germany, and some foodstuffs, such as cheese, flour, tinned meat, soup and fruit were becoming scarce as the War Office assumed priority for wholesale orders. Many prices had increased soon after war broke out, hitting working-class families hard. Although the newspapers failed to indicate weights, during August 1914 lard suddenly rose from 7*d* to 8*d*, lentils from 2*d* to 4*d*, butter beans from 3.5*d* to 5*d*, granulated sugar from 2*d* to 4*d*, cheese from 7.5*d* to 10*d* and unsmoked bacon from 10*d* to 1/-. Nevertheless, a few months into the war grocers, greengrocers, butchers, tailors and drapers told the *Flying Post* they were still doing well. Too well, thought some people writing to the newspaper, accusing the city's retailers of profiteering.

Lifebuoy Soap advertisement. (Trewman's Flying Post, 5.6.15)

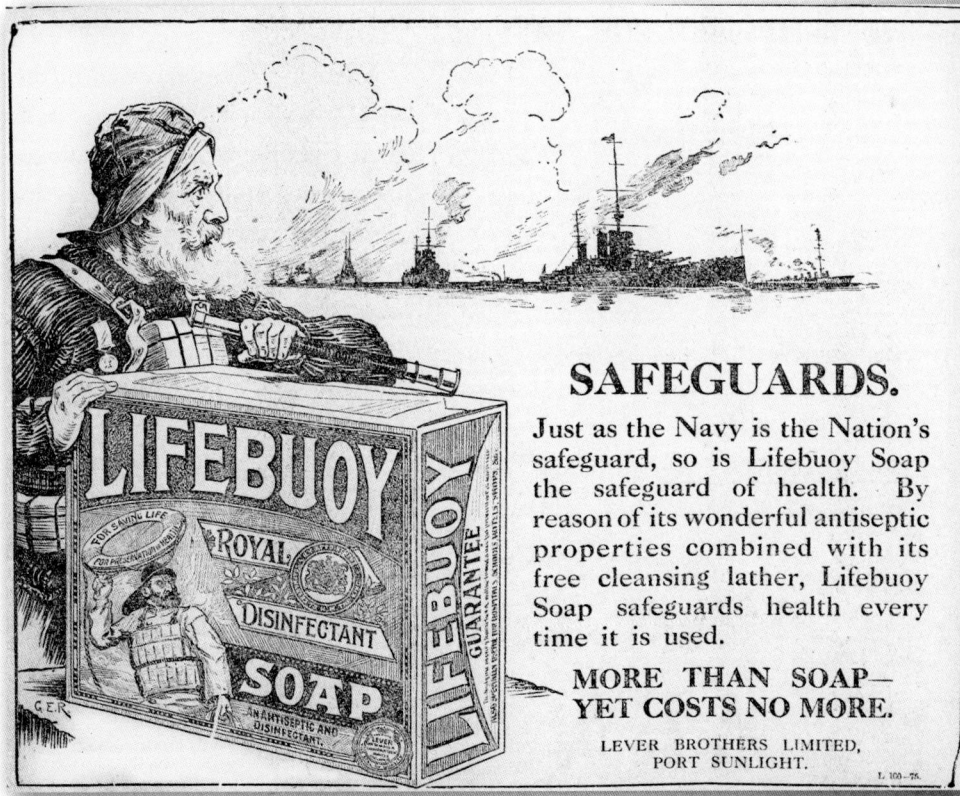

SAFEGUARDS.

Just as the Navy is the Nation's safeguard, so is Lifebuoy Soap the safeguard of health. By reason of its wonderful antiseptic properties combined with its free cleansing lather, Lifebuoy Soap safeguards health every time it is used.

MORE THAN SOAP— YET COSTS NO MORE.

LEVER BROTHERS LIMITED, PORT SUNLIGHT.

Throughout the war, the manufacturers of household goods lost no advertising opportunity to tell housewives that patriotism demanded their particular products were purchased. Incorporating military and naval images into advertisements was believed to bring comfort and confidence to potential consumers; Ven-Yusa was sure its face cream would restore 'sweet freshness' to the complexions of women war workers. There were few shortages at Christmas 1914 and, as always at that time of the year, advertisements proliferated for a host of alluring gifts. The railway companies announced Christmas excursions to London, Winchester, Salisbury and Weymouth, and J & G Ross proudly announced, 'In spite of the war we have the latest designs from Paris.'

The 'Maxim' worker advertisement. (Trewman's Flying Post, *8.4.16*)

The 'Maxim' worker.

VIM does the maxim-um amount of work in the minimum length of time. Brightness after Brightness follows its use in rapid succession. It's very deadly on DIRT, RUST and TARNISH. Try it for your bright metals, clean all your paintwork, tilework and enamel with it. Keep your knives ever bright and clean with it. A little VIM on a damp cloth is all you require.

DON'T APPLY THE VIM DRY.

IN SPRINKLER-TOP TINS OF THREE SIZES.

LEVER BROTHERS LIMITED, PORT SUNLIGHT.

In 1915 the standard of living for most families was not under threat. The families of serving soldiers received war allowances and those billeting the 3,000 extra soldiers in the city received further weekly payments. However, in an acid comment upon the alleged generosity of the allowances and some working-class women's attitudes, in March 1915 the *Flying Post* claimed the following exchange was overheard at Queen Street station:

'Well, I be getting 18s a week; how much do you get?'

'Why, 27s a week, but then you know, I've got children. You know Mary Ann Parsons? Well, she says she hopes the war'll last for ever, as she never had so much money in her life.'

Just as both retailers and shoppers witnessed wartime changes in demand, supply and prices, so other aspects of citizen's lives continued unabated but with significant wartime differences. Exeter's Theatre Royal and the Palladium and Palace cinemas never faltered in their attempts to fill their seats, often by using American productions. In early January 1915, the Palladium showed *Tess of the D'Urbervilles*, and *Mother Goose* was the seasonal pantomime at the Theatre Royal. Soon afterwards the theatre put on an early American musical called *The Marriage Market*, in which a wealthy senator's daughter inadvertently marries a cowboy and her poor friend marries an English aristocrat.

Wreford's Christmas 1914 advertisement. (Trewman's Flying Post, 19.12.14)

Ven-Yusa face cream advertisement. (Western Times, 31.10.18)

*Theatre Royal,
London Inn Square.
(Dr Sadru Bhanji)*

In June 1915, massive publicity was given to 'D.W. Griffith's Mighty Spectacle "The Birth of a Nation" from the United States'. A suitably patriotic poster thundered, 'SEE the Regeneration of a Nation, as England will be reborn when the War is over.' That November, citizens could enjoy Charlie Chaplin films at the Palladium, the salaciously titled *A Delayed Reformation* and *In Satan's Toils* at the Palace, and the drama *The Pearl Girl*, 'brought straight from London', at the Theatre Royal.

Patriotic concerts and traditional revues were staged regularly at various venues. In April 1915, for example, the 'Smart Set', annual visitors to Devon's resorts, put on a programme of songs, dances, impressions and sketches at King's Hall in St Thomas. National celebrities came down from London. In January 1915, Madame Clara Butt entertained audiences at Victoria Hall with a repertoire of classical and patriotic songs, and the celebrated impersonator Vesta Tilley did the same in August 1916. Both 'stars' were well known for encouraging recruitment.

Forthcoming features at the Palladium Cinema, Paris Street, September 1914 (Trewman's Flying Post, 19.9.14)

The cinemas were quick to combine comedies and melo-dramas with films of recent battles, either recreated by actors or claimed to be of the actual events. In September 1914, the Palladium featured the devastation of several Belgium cities; in February 1915, *The Bells of Rheims* told the story of the cathedral's total destruction; and in September 1916, *The Battle of the Somme* showed the various heavy guns, the infantry assault, men falling, mines bursting, the ground littered with the dead, the wounded receiving treatment, and the lines of prisoners.

Other glimpses of lighter moments in the city appear along-side the films, plays, concerts and revues. In February 1917, the River Exe froze hard enough for skaters to take to the ice. League football matches might have faded away as enlistment decimated many teams and commentators thought such aggressive plebeian entertainments inappropriate in wartime, but the city's cycling clubs still arranged

"GERMAN ATROCITIES!"

A FILM TAKEN ON THE SPOT, showing the frightful devastation of Termonde and Melle,

CAN BE SEEN AT THE

PALLADIUM

(PARIS-STREET)

MONDAY, Sept. 21st, and Two Following Nights.

7—TWICE NIGHTLY—9

Don't miss seeing this picture, reported to be the best war film yet so far produced. Also up-to-date Picture and Variety Programme.

Important Engagement of

SABLE THREE AND SEARLE

in a novel and refined Comedy, Dancing and Singing Speciality.

First Visit of

ELSIE SEYMOUR,

Charming Comedienne.

SPECIAL PICTURE FOR MONDAY—

"NO QUARTER,"

A very Powerful Drama. Exciting, Sensational.

"OUR BI-WEEKLY GAZETTE." All best war pictures.

Popular Prices: 1s, 9d, 6d, & 3d.

HELP A GOOD CAUSE!

Grand Benefit on FRIDAY, Sept. 25th, in aid of the

BELGIUM RELIEF FUND.

Specially Augmented Programme. See Bills.

healthy outings, motorcycling groups still toured Dartmoor, the swimming baths still organised galas, and a number of tourist businesses found they could reopen when a sprinkling of summer visitors started to return in 1915. People with a few silver coins in their pockets could enjoy a sophisticated hour or so enjoying refreshments in the wondrously gilded surroundings of the new Dellar's Café that opened in the High Street in 1916,

Jack Frost Delights the Young.

DURING the past week skating has been greatly in vogue at Exeter, owing to the River Exe and the Canal being frozen over for the first time for many years. Large numbers have also watched the sport from the banks. A favourite spot has been on the Canal, adjoining and immediately below the Double Locks Hotel, where there was a fine stretch of ice. The first photo shews a couple of skaters executing a combined movement at this spot. Higher up the canal, and near the first drawbridge, there was also a fine run, and here some children are seen merrily disporting themselves. Wednesday, being half-holiday, was fully taken advantage of, and there were some merry scenes on the river. Hundreds also gathered on the ice in the evenings, the moonlit scene being exceedingly novel and picturesque.

Skaters on the frozen River Exe. (Western Times, 9.2.17)

complete with terraces, dance floor and resident musicians despite the exigencies of war. It became the centre of Exeter society. Convalescing soldiers saw it as somewhere special, but also, as one perceptive amateur poet recalled, somewhere where local snobbery was a little too obvious.

Later on, though, household economies were avidly encouraged as the army appropriated more supplies, the U-boat campaign intensified, import slumped and raw materials for domestic goods became scarce. In the summer of 1916, Board of Trade figures showed that between July 1914 and June 1916 the overall cost of food had risen 65%, clothing 55%, and fuel and lighting 40%. Earlier in the year the *Western Times* had noted the local increases in the price of bread, meat and poultry. In November 1916, Exeter's War Savings Exhibition successfully attracted public attention when a group of soldiers pushed a captured German Fokker biplane complete with two machine guns and a bomb rack through the streets to Victoria Hall where it was placed on display alongside an artillery piece, a sniper's gun and bits of a Zeppelin. Visitors flocked to see the relics of war, and then presumably stayed to tour the domestic exhibits and demonstrations.

Dellar's Café.
(Dr Sadru Bahnji)

DELLER'S CAFÉ · EXETER

It was a big and eclectic event, showing citizens how to keep poultry, grow herbs, use gas and electric appliances economically, and carry out first aid effectively. Demonstrators also pointed out how families could cut down on the servants they needed through the use of new powered geysers, cookers, irons and radiators. Coming full circle, it went to show how their savings, suitably invested in government war bonds, could provide 'shells, fuses, steel helmets, bombs and other things for strafing Huns'.

DELLAR'S.

A little V. A. sat on a wall,
And called to a friend below,
" Say, what do you think of Dellar's for tea,
The cost to be borne betwixt you and me?"
And the other one said " Right O !"

So off they went to St. Martin's Lane,
And ordered a sumptious tea,
And while they ate it, a fearful band,
Of three musicians, made music grand,
Conducive to felo de se.

And oh the sights that met their eyes,
As shyly they gazed around,
V. A.'s in plenty, and Cadets too,
(A munching, laughing, noisy crew,)
And ladies wonderfully gowned.

Three sour old Dowagers, tabby cats,
A sweet young thing in blue,
A grumpy Colonel, his wife in tow,
A khaki Parson who fears no foe,
All jostle and hurry through.

The din and racket and heat and smell,
An indescribable whole,
So far from making their heads to ache,
Increased their enjoyment of tea and cake,
And they called for another roll.

" Time's up !" they cried, with an injured sigh,
And trotted away to Five,
Refreshed and happy, their " souls " at rest,
They did their duty with strength and zest,
Like two worker bees in a hive.

A soldier's poem, 'Dellar's'. (Devon Heritage Centre)

The city included many open spaces and by early 1917 most of them had been turned into vegetable allotments. Hundreds of plots were created on the 2.5-acre public park adjoining Ladysmith School in Heavitree, on St Luke's Teachers' Training College sports field, on part of Veitch's nursery in St Davids, on the site of demolished houses in Blackboy Road and on unused ground at Exwick Cemetery. There was a great rush of applicants, and the city council provided tools and seed potatoes at cost price. Sadly, most of the potatoes that year were lost to disease, and to the popular belief that chemical spraying stopped them keeping and adversely affected the flavour.

In June 1917, the city's Food Control Campaign Committee opened its High Street Bureau opposite the Guildhall. Here, under a banner inscribed 'The Kitchen is the Key to Victory', regular demonstrations were held of dishes using economical ingredients and the newly introduced war rations. Among the new dishes were those using meat substitutes. They included curried haricot beans, rice and cheese pie, and a pudding made from oatmeal, suet, onions and sage.

Women queuing for potatoes. (Western Times, 9.3.17)

The New Craze—Potato Hunting.

THE "Western Times" photographer, one day this week went out potato hunting, with a basket in one hand and a camera in the other. That is how he chanced to 'snap' this small crowd, every member of which is eagerly waiting for his or her share of the "rare and refreshing" vegetable.

From April 1917, the city's cafés and restaurants had to cope with the government ban on offering light pastries, muffins, crumpets and teacakes for sale, and the severe restrictions on the amount of flour and sugar that could go into cakes, biscuits, buns and scones. In December that year, agitated and unruly queues formed outside shops selling butter and margarine, and when a pannier market dealer eventually secured a supply of butter near Christmas, 1,000 people received just ½lb each, and many latecomers had to leave empty-handed. The shortages continued in 1918.

In February 1917, the city's greengrocers and market traders ran out of potatoes. There was a poor harvest, but (probably justified) suspicions also abounded that farmers and wholesalers were holding on to stocks to force the government to raise the current price ceiling of ½d a pound. By March there were long queues outside shops as soon as rumours circulated that supplies were about to arrive. When a trader in St Thomas eventually secured half a ton, he sold them in 2lb lots 'while a burly policeman regulated the crowd with difficulty' and a 'sturdy trolley' was held between the trader and the desperate crowd.

The government's attempts at price control also caused a shortage of meat in early 1918. Imports had fallen sharply due to the ravages of German submarines, but it was the government's huge purchase of cattle in 1917, coupled with its progressive lowering of maximum retail prices, that led farmers to realise the following year that holding back sales was calculated to push prices up. In the meantime, families suffered. Turkeys, geese, chicken and ducks were reported to be way beyond the reach of Exeter's 'poor classes' at Christmas, and only fatty pork joints were cheap.

In October 1917, twenty-four embarrassed residents and shopkeepers faced Mayor Owen at the Police Court, charged with buying and selling sugar in contravention of the National Sugar Commissioner's Order. Sugar remained very scarce until early 1918 and it could be bought only for making jam or preserves from fruit grown on trees and bushes owned by the purchaser. And none of those before the Bench grew any, said the Chief Constable. The following month, seven more cases were heard, with fines ranging from 10/- to £1 depending, it seems, on the amount of sugar fraudulently purchased. The Order made shop-keepers as guilty as customers if the law was broken. As a pointed *Punch* cartoon reprinted in the *Flying Post* revealed, the Order was not altogether fair as expensive chocolates could be freely sold, but not relatively cheap sugar.

By January 1916, an average of 114 people were turning up each day for the city's Farthing Breakfasts, but funds to subsidise them were drying up. The farthing cost was deliberate, as it distanced the recipient from the hateful taint of pauperisation. In February 1917, a soup kitchen reopened in Lower Market. In addition to adults, 500 children frequented it and many of them missed school to ensure a place in the queue. As a result, it was decided to issue them with tickets so they could stay at school knowing they had priority when the doors opened. A total of 1,400 gallons were given away each week. In May 1917, a communal kitchen opened in Exe Island Mission Hall, run by the Exeter Food Control Campaign Committee, mainly comprised of city councillors. The aim was to provide good-quality meals at low cost through the bulk purchase of components, thereby saving working-class families money, fuel and time, as well as avoiding any hint of charity or pauperism. It was heavily promoted as a war economy with attendance being a sign of patriotism. The *Western Times* listed the substantial dishes:

Tuesday:	Baked Hot Pot & Milk Pudding
Wednesday:	Soup & Baked Date Pudding
Thursday:	Savoury Soup & Baked Jam Roly-Poly
Friday:	Soup & Baked Currant Pudding
Saturday:	Soup & Meat and Vegetable Pudding

In June 1915, Exeter's Board of Guardians moved into their grand new offices in Southernhay. They had cost several thousand pounds and were heavily criticised. The *Western Times* stoked the fires of controversy by describing the extensive wooden panelling and comfortably upholstered chairs, disingenuously noting that the Guardians had found their Castle Street rooms 'inconvenient and objectionable'. With some insensitivity, just before the inaugural

*Cartoon on the vagaries of the Sugar Order. (*Trewman's Flying Post, *2.12.16)*

meeting the Board had decided to reduce the meat ration and suspend the weekly bacon dinner for workhouse inmates. And on New Years Day 1916, they decided there was no need for extra free coal to be distributed, with one member thinking his colleagues were 'being led astray by the Christmas spirit' for suggesting it. That summer, they discussed whether local servicemen who became lunatics should be legally pauperised by incarceration in the workhouse and the idea was unanimously opposed. The Guardians decided pauperisation was unfair on the soldiers and, more pertinently, unfair on ratepayers notwithstanding the modest government grant attached to lunatic inmates, and they joined the widening campaign amongst Guardians to make the War Office accept responsibility. It was an interesting comment on the increasing prevalence of wartime shell shock, and the army's enduring reluctance to admit its extent, or even its existence.

The war had a significant impact upon children. Many suffered the absence and loss of fathers and brothers, but to some extent the war enlivened as much as it disrupted their schooldays. As we have seen, at least three large schools were requisitioned and the pupils relocated across the city. The inevitable economies led to school closures. Early in 1915, the small Exe Island Girls' School closed and the ninety-nine children were distributed between St Thomas, Okehampton Road and St Mary Arches schools. Thirty-one of the seventy-four male elementary school teachers had enlisted by July 1916 and a number of classes were amalgamated to cover the losses in staff. In some schools, temporary female 'war supply' teachers were employed instead but, according to the headteacher at St Thomas' School, several proved to be less than satisfactory. By early 1916, no more maps and atlases, or reading or library books, could be purchased and every scrap of paper had to be used. The gutting of the large Okehampton Road Girls' and Infants' School by fire in February 1917 caused disruption not only to its own teachers and children but also to Cowick Street School and St Thomas' Boys' School, which had to be completely reorganised to take the displaced classes of girls. Fortunately the empty Exe Island School building became a temporary refuge for the Okehampton Road infants.

Great efforts were made to ensure that children not only understood Britain's role and purpose in the war, but also supported it wholeheartedly. Through sales of work, penny collections and patriotic concerts, schools contributed money to the War Refugees Committee, emergency hospitals and Prisoners of War Fund. They also knitted garments for Devon Regiment troops and collected eggs for the hospitals.

Empire Day – 24 May – became the most important anniversary in the school year and was heavily laden with martial and religious overtones. The mayor, clergy and city councillors visited schools to stress the achievements of past Empire-builders and the need to preserve the nation's worldwide God-given territories against all aggressors. Britain's duty towards the people in the Empire, although it was never specifically defined, now transcended any thoughts of exploitation of their countries. In all the schools, pupils marched around the playground or a nearby field and smartly saluted the Union Jack as they passed it by. They sang patriotic songs such as 'Hearts of Oak', 'Sons of the Motherland', 'Drake's Drum', 'Land of Hope & Glory', 'Rule Britannia' and 'Where are the Boys of the Old Brigade'. Prayers and the national anthem were obligatory. The loyalty of the Dominions and colonies was given an honourable mention, but primarily 24 May was about Great Britain's glorious Empire and the children's – especially the boy's – future duty to defend and develop it. Trafalgar Day – 21 October – was also significant in instilling in children the Royal Navy's continuing role in maintaining the Empire, ensuring the free flow of British trade, and destroying any foreign invasion fleets – whether they were Spanish, French or German – long before they reached our shores.

From 1916 onwards, Exeter schools took part in the annual nationwide collection of horse chestnuts. The reason was kept secret, but they had been found to be an alternative

THE COUNTRYSIDE COLLECTIONS

Horse chestnuts were gathered everywhere, but rural children made other forays. The sweet tooth of soldiers led children to collect blackberries for jam. They received 3*d* per lb. More valuable were Devon's wild whortleberries, picked for jam but also as a source of blue dye. And Devon families gathered sphagnum moss in the waterlogged hills and valleys. Its spongy and slightly anti-septic properties made it ideal for turning into absorbent dressings for wounds.

to grain and wood, both in very short supply, in the distillation of acetone, a vital component in the manufacture of the explosive cordite. Their destination was kept secret, too, but it was a factory in distant King's Lynn. The children scoured the city's parks, gardens and surrounding countryside. On 17 October 1917, Heavitree Parochial School proudly recorded its total of three hundredweight. Elsewhere, several boys were caught throwing chestnuts at passing vehicles, and when a group was chased out of a garden in Cowick Street, 12-year-old Archibald Raymond caught his foot jumping over the wall and later died from the injuries.

Children were also found to be useful propaganda agents. Schools urged them to convince their families of the benefits of National Savings Certificates and War Bonds, and many head-teachers started Savings Banks. A government pamphlet entitled 'A Talk to School Children on Our Daily Bread' explicitly linked eating less bread and consuming every crumb with saving the lives of merchant seamen, defeating Germany sooner rather than later, and avoiding being greedy and careless and possibly arrested as a traitor. The children were told to tell their families all about it. A pamphlet calculated to arouse great excitement and a frisson of fear was entitled 'The Inadvertent Disclosure of Military Information'. In chilling terms, it warned children against telling anyone they did not know anything about what was going on in the locality. Disobedience could result in widespread death and destruction. With the endless spy scares, no doubt many children took the message to heart. Certainly John Stocker, chairman of the education committee, took it seriously, noting how often he had heard travellers on the trams gossiping about military matters.

Despite the children's good work, as the war entered its second year city magistrates bemoaned what they believed to be the rising incidence of juvenile crime, notably theft from cars, shops and allotments, and throwing stones at houses, horses, trains and passers-by. Some blamed the cinemas, asserting the thefts were to get the entrance money, with the inclination to act criminally stemming from imitating villains in the films.

A FEW CASES FROM EXETER POLICE COURT

5 February 1916:
Two boys birched for stealing and selling chickens, and stealing rent from their mother to play on slot machines.

25 September 1917:
Five boys aged 11–14 fined for throwing horse chestnuts at trains and houses in Pinhoe Road. Their mother said the teachers who had asked for the chestnuts should have supervised the collection.

15 January 1917:
Boy aged 13 birched for stealing a watch from a motorcar parked briefly in Southernhay.

2 July 1918:
Six boys aged 9–13 fined 1/- and 2/- for throwing stones at a horse in Water Lane.

One city councillor claimed that children's minds become 'familiarised with death, crime, killing, and other forms of unnatural and undesirable excitement', and the council agreed that censorship would be a good thing. One celebrated case in 1918 seemed to confirm their worst suspicions. A dozen boys, aged up to 15, took to wearing black masks as the Silken Cord Gang, and enjoying themselves verbally abusing pedestrians and breaking into several lock-up shops until they were eventually cornered at St David's station.

Others blamed the lure of the city's numerous slot machines. The head-teacher of Rack Street Central Boys' School, however, had another idea. In January 1917, after glumly recording the early enlistment of three masters and observing the steadily rising number of canings in school for bullying, fighting, lying, rudeness to teachers and truancy, and the police birchings for theft and vandalism, he was convinced that: 'The absence of fathers on military service, in conjunction with habits of drinking, gossiping and idleness on the part of some of the mothers is having a disastrous effect on the behavior of the children.' Exeter's Chief Constable and the headmaster of the city's Industrial (later Approved) School fully supported the magistrate's policy of publicly naming and shaming recalcitrant culprits, and thereby the parents, and ordering a salutary birching or a period of internment with strict discipline. Otherwise fines of several shillings were usually imposed on offenders, but there was rarely any consideration of probation or signs of sympathy with city families under severe wartime pressures.

Certainly an ever-growing number of families were without their menfolk. Conscription was more and more 'in the air' during 1915 as volunteering plummeted, and finally it came in May 1916. However, the Act permitted men to apply for exemption from military service on grounds of conscience – the 'conscientious objectors' – as well as extreme family or business pressures. Few people sympathised with conscientious objectors and cases in Exeter reveal the difficulties the applicants experienced facing the city and district's tribunal: comprising Mayor James Owen, two or three other aldermen and senior councillors and the army's representative. In July 1916, R.C.T Hart, a young watchmaker at Brufords, vainly sought exemption as a pacifist but made the mistake of saying that earlier in the war he had applied to 'do ammunition work'. Immediately he was asked, 'You are ready to make the cartridge to put in the rifle, but not to pull the trigger?' And when he claimed the Bible said he should not commit murder, he was charged with the counter-argument that the Bible did not say killing was a mortal sin under all circumstances. Such a faltering case, or one where nerves simply overcame the applicant, stood little chance of success.

W.J. Pedlar, aged 18, a chemist's assistant, was also rejected, but conversely because he seemed too confident and loquacious. He was a Socialist, he claimed, and believed in the brotherhood of man, irrespective of nationality. Killing was wrong and doing anything to assist another person to kill was equally wrong. Pedlar's fervent defence of Socialism and his denial of adherence to any Christian group were unlikely to gain sympathy. Nevertheless, he maintained his defence against all opposition and threats. His appeal failed and, in December 1916, he was court martialled in Plymouth for refusing to put on his uniform and then imprisoned. When sentenced he said that he trusted his stand 'would do a little, at least, towards heralding the dawn of international Socialism'.

> **RACK STREET SCHOOL LOGBOOK: 19 OCTOBER 1917**
> I punished G. Flynn and W. Jones for truanting. Yesterday they went off, leaving a note at home to say they had gone away. They only had a bundle of food, a penny and a lantern between them. At night they were put on a train at Crediton and sent back to Exeter by a lady who found them there.
> *(Headmaster's entry)*

Some weeks earlier Lawford Evans, an Exeter University College student, had found his Church of England membership offered no protection when he added provocatively that 'conscience was a delicate touchstone not to be judged by any tribunal composed of humans'. Indeed, it merely allowed the chairman to tell him he would have to do what other members of the Anglican Church were doing – go to war. And in February 1917, Bertie Seldon, a tram driver, met only contempt when he admitted his conscientious objection had come upon him when his application and appeal on the grounds of having three young children and a delicate wife had failed.

In June 1918, Alfred Chandler, a photographer in the Arcade, probably knew his application was doomed. He had served two months in prison under DORA for distributing Union for Democratic Control leaflets entitled 'What are we fighting for?' that argued that tens of thousands were dying in a war caused by capitalist profiteers and their political henchmen. Exeter's magistrates had found his actions appalling, and the tribunal had no sympathy with his pacifism, or his accusation that 'you have made widows and orphans galore'.

A small number of conscientious objectors across Devon whose applications and subsequent appeals failed still refused to have anything to do with the war as a soldier, or if it was offered, as a farm labourer or member of an army non-combatant labour unit. They ended up before courts martial at Higher Barracks in the city, and were then imprisoned after the inevitable guilty verdict. Among them was Thomas Bailey, an Exeter dairyman. Tried on 30 June 1916, on 4 July he was marched onto the parade ground in front of 100 or more fully uniformed and armed troops where the guilty decision was read out and a sentence of a year's imprisonment with hard labour imposed. City newspapers carried detailed reports of the men's humiliation, and accompanying editorials invariably condemned them as 'objectionable cranks' and traitors.

The newspapers could count on most readers' support. Indeed, if the conscientious objectors' arguments were right, the mounting sacrifice of so many men and their families would, by definition, be wrong and worthless. For most people that was too terrible a thought to contemplate, and of course the newspaper editors knew it.

The city tribunal's sympathy tended to be limited to those with the direst domestic hardship or business difficulties, especially ones that might directly affect city life. In 1916, a fitter was exempted as only eight out of the original sixteen fitters in the large High Street company were left. The city manager of the Cathedral Dairy, the only man of military age now left there, was exempted, and his case was helped by the large number of women it now employed. The same factors allowed the manager of a wholesale wool company to secure exemption. And as thirty-six men from Heavitree Brewery had already enlisted, and women had replaced seven of the eight clerks, the tribunal released three of the five men who were now called up. A man, who now ran a 4-acres plant nursery, kept six cows and ran a coal yard singlehandedly also secured exemption. Many others without such obviously threatening circumstances were refused. Shop assistants, office clerks and general labourers were especially prone to refusal, and often endured surprise and scorn that they even had the temerity to apply.

After the war the *Western Times* published the Exeter Tribunal's digest of its work and confirmed Sir James Owen's great satisfaction with it. In January 1918, the mayor's long wartime tenure of office had been marked by a knighthood in the New Year's Honours List. In all, 148 meetings of the tribunal had been held and 6,028 decisions made, of which only 477 had gone to appeal where 379 of the original decisions had been upheld. Sir James was particularly pleased that only eighteen conscientious objectors had been exempted, and of these only four exempted from military work altogether. He was gratified that relations with the military representative on the tribunal had been consistently good. He believed the tribunal members' detailed local knowledge had enabled hard-pressed but vital city businesses to function satisfactorily while ensuring the armed forces secured their full quota of men.

CONSCIENTIOUS OBJECTORS

Almost 16,500 men were recorded as conscientious objectors once conscription was introduced in 1916. Of these some 4,000 were sent to do civilian work of 'national importance', and 6,500 were ordered into non-combatant military units, largely responsible for construction and support work behind the front line but also providing stretcher-bearers and first-aiders nearer to the front.

However, 6,000 were forced into the regular army when their applications and subsequent appeals had been rejected. A minority of these men refused to be medically examined, to don uniforms or to obey military orders, and were eventually court-martialled and sentenced to terms of imprisonment.

Conscientious objectors were widely perceived as cowards, slackers and traitors, and frequently condemned as such, especially by serving soldiers and their families. However, a few who talked seriously with them or witnessed the bravery of stretcher-bearers took a more measured approach to the complex issue.

In 1917, Dartmoor Prison changed its status and became a Work Settlement for several hundred conscientious objectors released from prison. The men had to work but they were free to leave the Settlement at certain times, and many wandered into local towns where they incurred considerable hostility. Several local councils, such as Okehampton, South Molton and Totnes, petitioned the Home Office to be placed out of bounds to these unwanted visitors. The men were accused of preaching atheism and republicanism, but on the other hand persistent stories of wilful ill treatment in the prisons and at the Settlement crept into newspapers and prompted questions in Parliament.

Devon's newspapers relished all the incidents of alleged abuse and local complaint. And many readers no doubt welcomed the open letter by the bishop, Lord William Cecil, who visited Dartmoor and then charged the conscientious objectors with being malcontents and revolutionaries who ate their 'generous rations' and enjoyed the Devon countryside while all the time plotting to bring bloodshed and ruin to the nation.

The entrance arch and gateway into Dartmoor Prison. (Author's collection)

6

COMING HOME

The year 1918 was another grim one. Few believed the Allies were winning when the year started and few believed it that summer.

August 1918 was the fourth anniversary of the interminable war and the cathedral held another service of intercession. Civic dignitaries, officers and troops from the barracks, and detachments of Boy Scouts, Girl Guides and Army and Sea Cadets crowded in alongside war-weary families. In the evening, 12,000 people from various Non-Conformist congregations gathered on the Cathedral Green for a non-denominational service and a speech from Sir James Owen. They were huge and sombre events, replete with hopes of national redemption, calls for divine intervention and appeals to personal steadfastness, but the reports hint at the sullen rather than uplifting atmosphere hanging over them.

As though the final brutal months of the war were not enough to endure, a new way to spread death and misery struck the country. The city's newspapers made little mention of the particularly frightening influenza pandemic that struck Great Britain that autumn, but across the world it killed far more people than the war itself, mainly through the pneumonia that took hold when the virus invaded the lungs. Doctors advised staying warm indoors and drinking plenty of fluids but, despite worthless advertisements to the contrary, little was known about the cause and there was no remedy.

ZIP *Advertisement for the cure of influenza.* (Truman's Flying Post, *1914-18*)

INFLUENZA AND COLDS CAN BE PREVENTED AND CURED BY

ZIP.

This is not an ordinary remedy by an means. It is quite different to anything else on the market, and when we say that ZIP DRIES UP A RUNNING COLD IN HALF AN HOUR OR CHECKS AND CURES INFLUENZA IN THREE HOURS, we merely state the truth.

SOLD IN BOXES AT 3s (postage 1½d)

A 3s box will cure a household, or act as a preventative for dozen people.

With the war entering a crucial stage, DORA placed a ban on news about the lethal nature and rapid spread of the disease, but a few clues exist about its deadly grip on Exeter. On 18 October 1918, a grim item in the *Western Times* announced the sudden death of 24-year-old Dorothy Prouse, a city tram conductress. She was, the report ominously declared, 'but one of the many victims which the influenza epidemic has claimed during the past few days in Exeter.' A week later, the street and house collections for 'Our Day' were badly hit. School logbooks reveal the desperate times too. Attendances at St Thomas' and Heavitree Parochial Schools, at opposite ends of the city, plummeted in late September and early October to less than 50% and the two schools, like most others, closed down for five weeks.

The Fatal 'Flu.

MISS DOROTHY (DOLL) PROUSE, of 24, Buller-road, St. Thomas, was but one of the many victims which the influenza epidemic has claimed during the past few days in Exeter. Miss Prouse succumbed to pneumonia, consequent upon the 'flu. In several other cases cardiac failure has been the result. Miss Prouse was conductress on the City Trams, and was very popular among the staff.

The Death of Dorothy Prouse.
(Western Times, *18.10.18*)

Finally, on 11 November 1918, headlines in the *Western Times* announced 'KAISER ABDICATES' and 'Crown Prince Renounces the Throne'. 'The last of the despots has gone,' it asserted, and then described the vicious rioting against the generals and imperial government in Berlin as Germany descended into chaos. In Exeter the day started quietly but nevertheless expectantly as peace negotiations had been had been underway for several days. Then, at 10.48 a.m., the notice was posted in the window of newspapers offices and 'They came in hundreds. Boys and children scampered waving flags and shouting; clerks left their stools and hurried out hatless; young lady shop assistants, hatless, too, came pell-mell scurrying to the scene.' Soon, 'each window in the main street fluttered a bold line of our national emblems, overlooking the joy of the surging crowd, as it streeled [*sic*] down the thoroughfares, its pent-up feelings at last finding vent and play'. The staff at Messrs Walton made and gave away hundreds of cocked hats made from paper Union Jacks. Wounded British, Australian and Canadian soldiers 'in their hospital blue went along arm in arm ringing a school bell, twirling a hand rattle, their adventures of [*sic*] the battlefield forgotten for the nonce'. By midday the crowds were dense, and the 'whole of the High Street was a slowly moving, parading throng'. Many women had tears of relief and joy streaming down their cheeks. Early in the afternoon 'confetti made its appearance in the streets, and soon the roadways were covered in it. The trams – all the trams which passed – were crowded and from them all streamed flags and favours.' More and more 'whistles, toy-trumpets and bugles' filled the air. And on top of a tram 'were twenty or so Colonials and wounded Britishers, their tunics and hats afire with Red,

White and Blue, as they sang and laughed and cheered'. In the middle of the afternoon, a procession of civic dignitaries, military personnel, bands, cadets, wounded soldiers and VADs had some difficulty in processing from Queen Street to the cathedral for a Thanksgiving Service, but the crowds good-naturedly parted for them, cheering and clapping. 'People stood packed together in the aisles, and sat around the pillars' during the service.

Afterwards the procession, and accompanying crowd, returned to Queen Street and stopped by General Buller's statue. Here Mayor Sir James Owen picked up the key threads of the Thanksgiving Service. 'We had done our best,' he said, 'but we knew we could not have smashed the "invincible" German Army unless God had been with us.' He reflected on the nation's pride in its armed forces and reverence for those 'who would never come back to us. Many of them lay upon the field of honour, glad to have given their lives for England and Empire. Let us remember in the years to come the sacrifices they had made because of the faith they had in this grand old England of ours (cheers).' A *Western Times* editorial commented, 'Never did the Mills of God seem to have done their work with such minute thoroughness.'

Not surprisingly, a combination of people's own bitter experiences and the constant propaganda engendered a widespread hatred of Germany and a fear that its relentless desire for European dominance would resurface unless it was permanently quashed. In the November Diocesan Letter, the Right Revd Lord William Cecil, Bishop of Exeter, asserted that 'The German is an absolute brute' and argued that measures should be taken 'to put it outside the power of Germany to

COLONIES AND DOMINIONS (EXCLUDING INDIA)

Men from around the Empire rallied to the Allied cause:

	Numbers serving	Numbers killed
Canada	458,218	56,639
Australia	331,814	59,330
New Zealand	112,223	16,711
South Africa	76,184	7,121
British East Africa	c.34,000	c.2,000
British West Africa	c.25,000	c.850
Ireland	c.135,000*	c.35,000
West Indies	15,600	†

*+50,000 in the regular army

†(The British authorities proved reluctant to allow them on active service overseas)

wreck the peace of Europe'. He explained, 'We confine madmen in asylums and savage animals in cages, not through a desire for vengeance but as reasonable safeguards.' His personal loss was great; three sons had been killed in battle.

Not everyone, though, demanded the everlasting humiliation of Germany. In April 1916, the city council formally agreed with a proposal sent to it, and other major towns and cities, not to trade with German and Austrian companies, or with companies with more than a third of their capital subscribed by Germans or Austrians, when the war was over. As some members argued, any future trading agreements would grievously dishonour the

The Rt Revd
Lord William Cecil,
Lord Bishop of
Exeter, 1916–36
(Devon Heritage Centre)

sacrifice of so many local lives. The vote was carried only by 25–22, much to the disgust of the rabidly anti-German city branch of the British Empire Union. Significantly, several council members were cautious about tying their successors to a vote they might not want to keep when peace was restored and business recovered.

Peace Day, 19 July 1919, was miserably wet in Exeter; it did not stop raining. Nevertheless it was the day marked for commemoration, if not exactly celebration, across the nation. On 28 June the Treaty of Versailles had been signed, formally ending the state of war between Germany and the Allies. The city's shops were decorated and sodden flags hung limply everywhere. In the morning, large parties of flag-waving schoolchildren converged on Broadgate from various directions and 1,500 of them attended another Thanksgiving Service in the cathedral. Lord William Cecil preached on the verse from Psalm 105 saying, 'Remember the marvellous works that He hath done,' and he declared that all the bravery of the troops and skill of the generals would have been in vain without God's blessing.

The Peace Day Parade. (Western Times, 24.7.19)

Victory March in Pelting Rain Thro' Exeter on Peace Day.

Later in the day the crowds watched a 1-mile long procession of men and women from every military and civilian force that had links with Exeter parade through the main streets from Higher Barracks. They marched down the High Street and Fore Street, through Commercial Road, Edmund Street, West Street and Coombe Street to South Street, Magdalen Street, Southernhay and Bedford Street and finally back along the High Street and Queen Street. There were several bands and 1,800 serving, discharged and demobilised soldiers, sailors and airmen from a variety of units, but notably the 1st, 2nd, 4th, 8th and 9th Devons, together with a convoy of wounded and disabled men. These were followed by units from the St John Ambulance Brigade, the VADs, Army and Sea Cadets, Boy Scouts and Girl Guides, the City Fire Brigade and several motor ambulances. Parties of distinguished guests sat with Lord Fortescue who took the salute at Bedford Circus and with Sir James Owen at the Guildhall. Afterwards 2,000 city dignitaries and servicemen sat down to lunch in the specially decorated Queen Street Market where Sir James and Lord Fortescue praised the valour of local servicemen and the wonderful work of the mayoress's depot in supporting them. They trusted that exactly the same devotion and determination shown in the war would see the nation successfully reinvigorated in peace. There was yet another battle to be won, they said, that of consolidating the Empire and restoring British commerce.

A few days later the wartime work of the VADs was commemorated in a packed cathedral. The dean praised the dedication of members in undertaking so many arduous and often humble tasks. Afterwards Lord Fortescue inspected the VAD contingents drawn up outside the cathedral and said their work might well not be over. He pinpointed the expansion of local nursing associations and the opening of the much needed pre-natal and child welfare clinics across the county.

In 1919, two ceremonies marked the end of the wartime labours of the Women's War Agricultural Committee. The first was held in Victoria Hall in February where speeches heaped praise upon the women who had worked on farms and in forestry. No mention was made of most Devon farmers' unusual reluctance to employ them, but at least a few farmers were present to acknowledge the women's skills and devotion to duty. The second, in the summer, marked Peace Day and signalled the end of the women's hard-fought battle to replace men on farms. Miss Calmady-Hamlyn, a leading campaigner, now announced that 'the last thing on their minds was to keep out the men when they came home'. Indeed, probably the last thing most women volunteers wanted to do was pursue peacetime careers as farm labourers. It was a far cry though from the striking recruiting rally the ambitious Women's Committee had organised in Exeter just a year earlier. In early 1918, when the shortages of both food and soldiers were acute, the city had been regaled with a huge procession headed by a banner with the slogan 'Women of Devon – the Nation's Food Supply Depends on You' and accompanied by the band of the 1st Devons. Following them were uniformed contingents of female farmworkers carrying spades, rakes and forks, units of the Women's Land Army and the Forestry and Forage Departments, together with twenty-five horses and assorted tractors, ploughs and wagons from the Devon Ploughing School at Woodwater Farm just outside the city. Lord Fortescue, Bishop Cecil and Sir James Owen had all in turn praised the women's zeal, highlighted the need to produce more food, ignored the farmers' prejudices against outside female labour and urged more recruits – forty of whom came forward.

The wartime work of Major Davis and Miss Buller was honoured, but on different occasions. During the 1919 Annual General Meeting of the Devon Red Cross Society, Lady Fortescue singled out Major Davis for particular praise and amidst great applause he was presented with an inscribed silver salver and a motorcar. In that year he was made a CBE, a Commander of the Order of the British Empire. It was higher than the MBE and OBE but not so illustrious as the DBE, the Dame Commander of the Order, that was bestowed upon Georgiana Buller. She had fallen seriously ill after the exertions of her wartime work, but in January 1920 many county digni-taries, including the Fortescues, assembled in Exeter to honour her work at the hospitals. Sir Henry Davy, Southern Command's consulting physician, spoke of the army's deep appreciation of her skills and efficiency, and Mrs Mildmay said how the men convalescing in her mansion at Flete had 'talked of the Exeter hospitals as "Paradise"'.

The war hospitals remained in military hands into 1919, much to the annoyance of John Stocker, the chairman of the education committee, who bemoaned the army's thoughtlessness towards the city's children. Other city aldermen and councillors had different priorities, though, and failed to support him: they welcomed the continuing extra trade and employment in the city. The fighting may have died away, but the army was still sending numerous soldiers back to England with debilitating illnesses such as malaria, tuberculosis and venereal diseases. The army released the Children's Home in March 1919 and Episcopal School that autumn, but kept the other buildings well into 1920.

Georgina Buller in later life. (Journal of Bone and Joint Surgery)

In January 1918, Lord Fortescue convened a meeting at Rougemont Castle to establish a county division of the Comrades of the Great War Association for discharged service personnel. The idea emanated from the Earl of Derby, the Secretary of State for War, and Colonel Wilfred Ashley, a Conservative MP and Grenadier Guards officer. They saw it as a more controlled and surreptitiously right wing alternative to the National Association of Discharged Sailors and Soldiers that targeted working-class men and had links with the Labour Party and Trades Unions, and also the National Federation of Discharged and Demobilised Sailors and Soldiers, which vigorously opposed the government's decision in 1918 to review the cases of men already exempted from active service and was agitating for far higher war pensions. At Rougemont, Lord Fortescue eulogised the unity of the nation in wartime, and optimistically said: 'Hardship and danger shared together, victories won together, had taught all that the wretched suspicions and clash of interests which divided them in the past were now no barriers to good fellowship or united work in a great cause.'

Other speakers explained that the Comrades Association existed to ensure members – which included officers as well as other ranks – received the pensions and allowances due to them, and drew comfort and support from attending the clubhouses that were to be established. It also existed, speakers said, to ensure the next generation never forgot the nation's wartime unity and sacrifices, and to promote the ideals of the British Empire that the men had fought so magnificently to preserve. Not surprisingly, an illustrious county committee was created to help establish and guide local branches. It included Sir Henry Lopes (ex-High Sheriff of Devon), Sir Earnest Cable (ex-Indian merchant and High Sheriff of Devon) Admiral Sir William Acland, Miss Georgiana Buller DBE and Major Davis CBE. With such prompting, the Comrades Association grew rapidly, and by October 1918 there were twenty-nine branches and 2,000 members across the county, excluding Plymouth that had its own division. An upbeat report from the Exeter branch showed its concern that members secured all the state pensions and allowances to which they were entitled. The Association stayed non-political – despite the efforts of several local candidates in the 1918 general election to ally themselves with the emerging branches. In 1921, the various rival organisations, together with the Officers' Association, merged into the Royal British Legion.

Many men found their service careers did not end with the Armistice, and Exeter had no general homecoming celebration. Many naval vessels stayed at sea and many army units stayed abroad. Prisoners of war were transported home in batches well into 1919 and the Mayoress of Exeter's Depot stayed open to ensure they had changes of clothing. At the end of 1918 the 2nd Devons marched past King George V at Tournai on

*'Devons' in India, 1919 (*Western Times, *3.1.19)*

Reading the "W.T." in India.

THE above snap of a group of West-country lads in India was sent to us recently by Pte. Gale, whose home is at Isca-road, St. Thomas, Exeter. "You will see that I have in my hand," writes Pte. Gale," a copy of the good old "Western Times," which was given to me by a friend who comes from Okehampton. Isn't it wonderful how the good old paper gets about." Pte. Gale wrote before the news of the Armistice had brought joy throughout the world, so that his hopes of an early return to the dear old City of the West are by now far nearer to realisation than then seemed possible. "I often think," he goes on, " of the kindness shown to us boys (of the 2nd Batt. Somerset Light Infantry) when we passed through Queen-street Station at 3 a.m. on March 15th, 1917, by the Mayoress of Exeter and her Committee. We enjoyed the refreshments, and I have still got the little card given to me then, and shall always value it. I often hear men from all parts speak the same. Well, every success to your well-known paper."

Band of the 2nd Devons at Tournai.

A FEW weeks ago we published a picture of the Band of the 2nd Devons marching past the King at Tournai on their way towards the Rhine. In the above photo, also taken at Tournai, individual members of the Band may be recognised. The group includes four Mons men. Reading from left to right, the members are: 1st Row— Bandsman C. Hentch, Corpl. Brian, J. Sharpe, Capt. Bowen, Major Horne, Sergt. de King, F. Bute, J. Channing, B. Knight. 2nd Row: Bandsman Davis, Corpl. E. Gurr, Pte. Winter, B. Turner, J. Stephens, Scragg, L-Cpl. E. Blunden, J. Cook. 3rd Row—Bandsman Midgly, R. Sanders, J. Hunt, Gray, A. James, P. Parker, J. Overton. 1st Row — Bandsman Murrant, Russell, A. Gibbs, A. Abbott, L-Cpl. Jones, M. Jenkins.

The band of the 2nd 'Devons' in Tournai before departing for Germany in 1919 (Western Times, 17.1.19)

their way to garrisons in Germany, not Devon. In January 1919, Pte Gale of the West Somerset Light Infantry wrote home to Isca Road in Exeter from India while still awaiting demobilisation, and in August the *Western Times* reported the 'further growls' coming from men in the 4th Devons in the Middle East who had not been selected for repatriation.

In July 1919, however, many of the men who had been fortunate enough to return from India and Mesopotamia assembled in Exeter for 'a smoking concert and reunion'. The speeches recalled their recent battles and colleagues killed, and the music included pieces such as Finck's musical memories and 'Nights of Gladness' that had been popular on active service. In the Commons, Winston Churchill, the Secretary of State for War, refused to be drawn on the garrisons in India, except to say that large forces had to be kept near troublesome Afghanistan. It was as part of this policy that in August 1919 800 men of the reconstructed 2nd Devons were cheered off at Devonport by Lord Fortescue, Sir James Owen and a large crowd for a three-year tour of duty in India.

DEMOBILISATION

A belated set of procedures governed the demobilisation of volunteers and conscripts. Those with much needed technical skills took priority, those who enlisted early were next and the 1918 conscripts were last. However, some regiments were sent to Germany and Russia or stayed on in India, much to many men's anger. Left in Wales until March 1919, some Canadians mutinied, but by the end of that year the British Army had reduced from 3.8 million to 900,000.

The Devonshire Regiment memorial in Exeter Cathedral. (Author's collection)

In October 1919, a couple of hundred of the Devons drawn from units in Exeter and Devonport returned from fighting the Bolsheviks alongside White Russian forces in the Soviet Union. Some were volunteers, some were not, but all of them had sailed to Murmansk that May as 'C' Company of the 1st Oxford & Buckinghamshire Light Infantry. To their amazement, parcels of warm clothing and toiletries from the Mayoress of Exeter's Depot were waiting for them. The men were stationed in the forests and swamps between the Vaga and Dvina rivers where there was no obvious front line, and units were forever striving to work out who was around them. Sniping took its toll, there was a plague of mosquitos, and the men quickly learnt not to trust the friendly overtures of civilians whose main ambition was to steal stores. One attack on a Bolshevik position was a costly failure due to the enemy's superior intelligence gathering and ferocious entanglements of barbed wire.

Exeter Cathedral – Bronze War Memorial to the Men of Devon.

TO THE GLORY OF GOD & IN MEMORY OF THE OFFICERS · WARRANT OFFICERS · N·C· OFFICERS & MEN OF THE DEVONSHIRE REGIMENT · WHO LOST THEIR LIVES DURING THE WAR 1914-1918

Several war memorials were erected in the city. Within the cathedral a large bronze sculptured frieze commemorates the dead of the Devonshire Regiment itself. It portrays a fully armed soldier kneeling amidst the ruins of a building and ready for battle. Behind him is a post holding a crucifix, the only thing left standing. The inscription says: 'To the Glory of God and in memory of the Officers, warrant officers, NC officers and men of the Devons who lost their lives during the war 1914–1918.' It was dedicated on 26 July 1921 but the 1919 campaign is not included as the men from the Devons were in a different regiment.

Another memorial, far less conspicuous and easily missed, adorns the west wall. Below the image of a wounded soldier being laid upon a stretcher, it lists the names of members of the Territorial battalions of the Wessex Field Ambulances who died between 1914 and 1919. Its inscription reads '*In arduis fidelis – usque ad mortem*' which is perhaps best translated as 'in times of peril faithful – even unto death'. It alludes as much to the proud military virtues of Ancient Rome as to Christianity. The men from these units were responsible for ensuring wounded men received basic treatment as quickly as possible and were passed from the front line through medical centres to hospitals, and, if necessary, back to the United Kingdom. The date '1919' shows that the names include those who died weeks or months after the Armistice as a result of their injuries or fell while serving in Russia.

On the Cathedral Green, to the west of its main doors, a monument remembers all those across the county who fell in the war. Despite the forthright condemnation of a monument as a 'useless waste of money' by the local chairman of the National Federation of Discharged Sailors and Soldiers, who much preferred any money to be spent on the dependents of fallen men, the County War Memorial Committee eventually agreed

WAR DEAD The slaughter of servicemen was prodigious:	
Germany	2,037,000
Austria-Hungary	1,100,00
Bulgaria & Turkey	892,000
Total Central Powers	4,029,000
France	1,398,000
British Empire*	198,000
United Kingdom	723,000
Russia	1,811,000
Italy	578,000
USA	114,000
Other Allies	599,000
Total Allies	5,421,000

*Outside UK

The county war memorial in Cathedral Close. (Tony Ovens)

that the likely sum it would raise, at most £2,000, would best be spent on a plain but dignified granite column. As Lord Fortescue, the chairman, acknowledged, each Devon town and village would be concentrating upon its own memorials and funds would be limited. Despite several alternative sites being proposed, such as Cawsand Beacon on Dartmoor and the Belvedere Tower on the Haldon Hills, the Cathedral Close in the county town became the generally preferred option. The Prince of Wales unveiled the memorial on 26 May 1921. During the ceremony Lord Fortescue stated that 11,600 men and women from across Devon had died on active service. He did not say how many had served. This is hard to determine, although one of Fortescue's unofficial calculations gives an estimated figure of 63,700 – comprising about 8,000 regulars, 36,700 volunteers and 19,000 conscripts.

The 2nd Devons memorial at Bois des Buttes. (Devon and Exeter Institution)

The County Committee also agreed to support the monument in France where the 2nd Devons had made their costly but vital stand the previous year.

The County Committee and Exeter War Memorial Committee conspicuously failed to work together on a joint memorial. According to a public letter written by Sir James Owen, the city sought a joint committee but the County Committee 'slammed the door in our face'. According to Lord Fortescue, the city had known the County Committee's wishes but decided to pursue its own plans without further discussion. The city certainly chose something entirely different. A strikingly ornate monument was erected high on the volcanic outcrop forming part of Northernhay Gardens where the presentations of captured guns, the Dominions' flags and so many bravery awards had taken place. Indeed, as late as August 1919, General Sir William Birdwood was there to award medals and to express the thanks of numerous New Zealander units to the Mayoress of Exeter's Depot for the station refreshments. With public subscriptions raising over £6,000, the locally born artist and sculptor John Angel created an allegorical figure of Victory with one hand holding a down-turned sword and the other offering a laurel branch – the ancient symbol of victory, rather than an olive branch of peace – to the heavens. A defeated and dead dragon lies at Victory's feet. The sculpture stands on a granite pedestal 20ft high and its base forms a cross. Each arm of the cross possesses a sculptured tableau representing a key feature of the city's war. In one a fully kitted soldier sits relaxed by a silent gun and appears quietly confident of his duty done. A second portrays a sturdy sailor at sea holding a chart and submarine net. He crouches astride a representation of a ship whose figurehead is Exeter's coat of arms. He suggests the ever-watchful Royal Navy, even though the war has ended. The third shows a stoical prisoner of war and recalls the work of the Mayoress of Exeter's Depot. The fourth represents a nurse holding a bandage. A shrapnel shell is nearby and so is a sheaf of corn, representing women's roles in war and the transition to peace. The Right Revd Robert Trefusis, the wartime scourge of the

The soldier, nurse, sailor and prisoner of war from the sides of the City of Exeter's war memorial in Northernhay Gardens. (Tony Ovens)

Shell Shock Cured.

LANCE-CORPL. JAMES H. MILLER, of the Devonshire Regiment, after lying helpless from shell shock for over two years, is back at his work at the Exeter General Post Office, sorting letters, less than three months after being taken on a stretcher to the Mount Pleasant Hospital, Chepstow, where he was cured by suggestion.

Germans, dedicated the memorial in July 1923, but the guest of honour who formally unveiled it was Admiral of the Fleet Earl Beatty, whose dashing personality and style of leadership made him a popular war hero despite the controversial role his battlecruisers played in the Battle of Jutland. By 1923, though, the vast majority of Germany's High Seas Fleet was safely rotting on the seabed at Scapa Flow. The memorial is neither jingoistic nor religious and although obviously sombre it possesses confidence; overall it suggests the city mourned its dead but also prided itself that the community as a whole had made a significant contribution to the nation's ultimate victory.

Perhaps three stories epitomise the pain and sadness that lingered long after the Armistice.

In January 1919, Police Sergeant and Mrs Perkins of Springfield Road still had no news about the fate of their son, a private in the Duke of Cornwall's Light Infantry, who went missing between 22 March and 2 April 1918 during the last German offensive.

In November 1919, L/Cpl James Miller tentatively returned to work at Exeter General Post Office 'after lying helpless from shell shock for over two years'. 'Suggestion', a simple form of psychotherapy, was said to have cured him. If his trauma had started in late 1917, it was at a time when the hard-pressed army and government banned shell shock as a diagnosis, and sought to return men to active service as soon as possible. He must have been fortunate in the doctors he saw, lucky not to be suspected of cowardice like so many shell-shock sufferers, and 'cured' was probably an over-optimistic claim for such an extreme case.

In May 1920, members of the Women's Section of the Exeter Branch of the Comrades of the Great War Association visited the Heroes Resting Place in Exeter's Higher Cemetery to attend a memorial service, and to care for the 180 graves of servicemen from across the world who had died in Exeter. They did this regularly and the rows of graves were still raw, much like, one feels, the sorrow, pride and anger of those who gazed upon them. Soon another stone column and cross would be erected there to remind future generations who lay nearby.

THE BODIES AND THE GRAVES

When the guns fell silent, the task of clearing battlefields and rebuilding communities began. The British Government decided to bury the dead near where they had fallen, partly because of cost and partly because so many could not be identified. By the 1930s, the Imperial War Graves Commission had created 918 cemeteries on the Western Front with 580,000 named and 180,000 unnamed graves. There were others in Italy, Gallipoli, Iraq, Palestine and the Balkans.

ON Saturday the members of the Women's Section of the Exeter Branch of the Comrades of the Great War visited Exeter Cemetery. They first held a short service at the Shrine (bottom picture), and then placed flowers and laurel wreaths (top picture) on the graves of the 180 soldiers, sailors, and airmen buried in the Heroes Resting Place.

Members of the Women's Section of the Comrades of the Great War Association attend a memorial service at the Heroes Resting Place in Exeter's Upper Cemetery, May 1920. (Western Times, *28.05.1920)*

THE PEACE TREATIES

The map of Europe was dramatically redrawn after the war. In May 1919 the Treaty of Versailles made Germany cede substantial territory to Belgium, France and newly created Czechoslovakia and Poland. Its colonies were placed under League of Nations mandates, Danzig became a Free City, and the Saar and the Rhineland fell under Allied control. Its armed forces were reduced to a few obsolete warships and a miniscule army. An air force was forbidden. A War Guilt Clause obliged Germany to accept responsibility for starting the war and pay huge reparations.

The Hapsburg's Austro-Hungarian Empire disappeared. In September 1919, the Treaty of Saint-Germain established the small Republic of Austria. Other Hapsburg lands were ceded to Italy, Poland, Czechoslovakia, Romania and the Kingdom of the Slovenes, Croats and Serbs (renamed Yugoslavia a decade later). The Treaty obliged Austria never to unite with Germany.

In November 1920 the Treaty of Trianon dealt with Hungary, the eastern half of the Hapsburg Empire. It survived as a small independent country, but had to cede Slovakia and Carpatho-Ukraine to Czechoslovakia, Transylvania to Romania, and several parcels of land to the Kingdom of the Slovenes, Croats and Serbs.

After an internal revolution, Turkey signed the Treaty of Lausanne in July 1923, which defined the borders of Turkey with Greece and Bulgaria, and ensured Turkey renounced all claims to ancient Ottoman lands in Europe and Africa.

The Allies had intractable problems to solve, and not surprisingly they created dangerous new ones. Many countries squabbled over their new borders, and popular opinion in Germany targeted the Treaty of Versailles as a 'dictated peace' and unbearably humiliating, thereby allowing Adolf Hitler to use the powerful argument of restoring German pride and territory as a platform for the advancement of the Nazi Party. Step by step he called the western Allies bluff, privately scorning their policy of appeasement, and thereby clawed back much of the territory lost in the war and massively expanded the armed forces.

The Exeter city war memorial. (Author's collection)

Postscript

Legacy

Less than a fortnight after the Armistice, Prime Minister David Lloyd George opened a General Election campaign on behalf of the Liberal and Conservative Coalition which, as agreed with Lloyd George and the Conservative leader Andrew Bonar Law, would continue to govern during the period of national recovery – if the electorate agreed. Lloyd George asserted, quite simply, that 'Our task is to make Britain a fit country for our heroes to live in'. To achieve this, he continued, many families must be enticed back to the land to increase agricultural production, new homes must be built – not old ones patched up – and everyone must be found work. He scorned the accusation that 'he was surrounded by reactionaries' and promised to return to the electorate if he encountered parliamentary obstruction.

Polling day was 14 December. It was the first election in which all men could vote, and all women over thirty as well. It resulted in a landslide victory for the Coalition with 332 Coalition Conservatives and 127 Coalition Liberals elected, who faced fifty-seven Labour MPs and thirty-six Liberals still loyal to the old Liberal leader, H.H. Asquith. There were also forty-seven Conservatives who were not formally labelled 'Coalition' MPs, seventy-three Sinn Fein MPs who refused to take their seats and thirty-five others who stood as various Independent Labour, Socialist, Liberal or Agriculturalist candidates. It seems the election had little to do with what might happen to defeated Germany, but represented widespread trust in Lloyd George's record as a war leader and his pre-war record as a social reformer who had introduced the National Insurance and Unemployment Insurance Acts when Chancellor of the Exchequer between 1908 and 1915.

Most, but not quite all, of Devon followed the national trend. In Exeter the Conservative Sir Robert Newman secured 12,524 votes against his Liberal opponent's 8,806, and Conservatives won back or easily held Barnstable, Tavistock, Tiverton, Totnes and Torquay, and the three Plymouth constituencies of Devonport, Drake and Sutton. George Lambert, the popular MP for South Molton since 1891, and a vigorous parliamentary voice on behalf of farmers, became the only Liberal member in the county.

SLUM CLEARANCE

In 1918 the housing shortage was estimated at 600,000. A succession of Housing Acts – in 1919, 1924 and 1930 – offered various incitements to local authorities, and despite the 'stop-go' nature of the economy over 1.5 million council houses were built between the wars. In Exeter many slums in the West Quarter were demolished in the 1930s and families moved to new homes in the old areas or on estates on the city fringes. Later decades have bemoaned the wholesale destruction of the ancient properties, and the lack of records.

The Coalition Government had achieved some much needed welfare reform during the war itself, and after the war further strides were taken. DORA, for all its oddities, had entrenched the idea of government centralisation and intervention for the general good of the nation firmly in people's minds. The 1919 Housing & Town Planning Act provided subsidies for local authority housing schemes, the 1920 Unemployment Insurance Act brought 11 million workers within the scheme, the 1920 National Health Insurance Act significantly extended pension rights, and the 1920 Employment of Women, Young Persons & Children Act prohibited the employment of children below the school leaving age in most industries. There were gaps and loopholes in these Acts but millions benefited from them.

It was the war itself that had brought about a marked change in attitudes towards mothers and young children. From 1915 onwards, shocking figures were prominently displayed in newspapers revealing that more babies and infants died each year than serving soldiers. And the relentless slaughter of young men led to a much higher value being placed upon the education and training of the rising generation, not least because vast armies and navies would be needed to defend Great Britain and its Empire in future wars.

Letters, lectures, public meetings and articles contributed to the campaign, all urging that the now unacceptable drain on the future workforce could be stemmed if pregnant working-class women were aided by maternity centres offering support, skilled advice and subsidised medicines and baby products. A Babies Welcome Club opened in Exeter 1908 with charitable and council funding to cater for cases recommended by the city's first health visitors. However, the city's first fully fledged Infant Welfare Centre opened in part of the disused Exe Island School building in early 1916. Over 100 mothers registered there in the first year and regularly attended the free surgery, and care and sewing classes. In April 1918, Lady Owen opened a new maternity home at No. 12 Dix's Field. It was run by the city's Nursing Association and supported by Exeter City Council, the city's Lying-In Charity and subscriptions.

THE 1918 EDUCATION ACT

When you get Conscription, when you get a state of affairs under which the poor are asked to pour out their blood and to be mulcted in the high cost of living for large international policies, then every just mind begins to realize that the boundaries of citizenship are not determined by wealth and the same logic that leads us to desire an extension of the franchise points also to an extension of education.

(H.A.L. Fisher, President of the Board of Education introducing the Education Bill in the Commons in August 1917)

The concept of a major Education Act, although not the detail, had originated in Lloyd George's mind soon after he became prime minister in December 1916. He saw it as a boost to public morale at a particularly depressing period of the war. The 1918 Act significantly extended the School Health Service and ensured local authorities established treatment services as well as regular inspections. It raised the minimum school leaving age to 14, without exemptions, and obliged education authorities to extend the provision of practical and vocational courses, and to organise compulsory part-time 'continuation classes' in a wide variety of subjects for young people up to the age of 16.

However the Act did nothing to narrow the social and educational divide between the elementary school system for working-class families and the largely fee-paying grammar schools for wealthier ones. Grammar school fees remained and no maintenance grants were provided for poor scholarship winners. Indeed, by enhancing the practical and vocational aspect of elementary education for essentially working-class children, the Act cemented its separateness from the more academically orientated grammar schools. It would take another world war to provide a free, universal and sequential system of primary and secondary education.

During the war, and increasingly when the Education Bill was 'in the air', the city council and education committee had devoted much time to debating whether there were enough city, charity and school-sponsored scholarships and bursaries – currently less than 50 among 8,090 children – to enable bright elementary school children to complete their education at one of the local grammar schools (Hele's, Maynards and the two Episcopal Modern Schools). There were also intermittent meetings around the city about the advancement of the small Royal Albert Memorial University College, which offered a host of courses at different levels in association with various trades, professions and awarding bodies, to independent university status. One suggestion was to call it 'Ralegh' University, another that it should combine with colleges in Plymouth and Cambourne to become the University of the South West. In the 1920s, a beginning was made on acquiring pieces of land and properties where the modern university now stands. In the 1920s and 1930s, as the fits and starts of the national economy allowed, the city took advantage of the Education Act to expand the School Health Service, provide more domestic science, handicraft and technical classes, and gradually increase the number of scholarships to grammar schools.

The pity was that within a couple of years of the Armistice, a worldwide economic depression led to severe cutbacks in national expenditure in all areas of domestic reform. For a brief period it looked as though a new golden age of full employment and widespread social reform had dawned, a fitting tribute to the nation's sacrifices, but massive over production led to the flooding of available markets, the stockpiling of unsold goods and the rapid collapse of prices, wages and jobs. Before the end of 1920, unemployment started to soar and the reform programme began to be rolled back as multiple government cutbacks were invoked. It was, though, the major manufacturing industries and towns that suffered most, although Devon, in common with all counties, felt the impact of the renewed railway and coal strikes.

Most history books surveying the 1920s see it as an era of rapid disillusionment, with the hoped-for rewards of victory failing to materialise. They highlight the swift return of misery and poverty for the working classes, the humiliation of the miserly 'dole' and the continuing distrust between the working classes and all the other sectors of society, despite the alleged and much vaunted unity displayed during the war. It was as though the noble and patriotic serviceman, praised to the skies during the war, was suddenly perceived as a troublemaker, even a revolutionary, when he replaced his uniform with overalls and his gun with a factory hand's spanner, coalminer's pick-axe or railwayman's oilcan. The citizen who had hitherto protected the nation so nobly now seemed bent on its destruction.

There is, of course, some truth is this view, but it is very much a partial one. Workers in the mines and heavy industries of South Wales, the Midlands and the North suffered badly, and everyone out of work struggled to make ends meet as the amount of state support was set at bare subsistence level. The stories, often true, of the massive profits businessmen made during the war, and the frequent charges of lies and broken promises hurled at the Coalition, made the post-war depression even harder to bear for families striving to cope with, and understand, the wartime sacrifices they had made. Few British men and women became members of the Communist Party but the alarms spread by middle-class commentators, the fears expressed by some government ministers, the dire threats made by the more extreme trades unionists and the lurid counter-accusations made by Conservative parliamentary candidates, all served to suggest that the country was falling into chaos, even civil war. Bolsheviks rather than German spies became the national bogey but the evidence suggests that Bolsheviks were as thin on the ground in Devon as German spies. Signalling the diversity but also the general bias of local opinion, two Exeter railway workers – known derisively as 'Comrade Lucy' and 'Comrade Porter' – who set themselves up as Communist agitators soon after the war were shouted down and chased by an angry mob through the back streets of the city when they tried to address a public meeting.

The newspapers recorded the unrest across parts of the country, and unemployment certainly rose in Exeter and other local towns. There were pockets of distress. In June 1920, Lord Fortescue felt obliged to send an open letter to all local newspapers saying that 2,000 Devon ex-servicemen, most of them young and able-bodied, were unemployed. They faced severely reduced unemployment pay and the dire threat of abject poverty, and he sought every employer's assistance in finding them work. It was a sop to public opinion, but full employment did not return until the end of the decade and then only to be hit by the depression of the early 1930s.

Nevertheless for those men in employment, which were the great majority in Devon, wages in wartime had outstripped prices, and as inflation stayed low in the 1920s most working-class families in the city found they had a little spare money for extras, such as weekly visits to the cinema or the seaside, further items of clothing, or better quality food. The High Street was buoyant with plenty of family businesses such as Colsons the drapers, Rush the florists, Hoskins the bakers, Lemmon the chemists, Wykes the photographers, Shapley the confectioners, Webbers the ironmongers and Lakes the gold and silversmiths, and of course numerous public houses and Dellar's Café. There was also Boots and Timothy Whites the chemists, the Maypole Dairy, and Fowlers, the National Provincial, and London Joint City and Midland Banks. The trams were busy and prosperous enough for a complete post-war refit in 1920. And the coastal cargo and pleasure traffic picked up, the summer passenger trains were crammed with holidaymakers, and the long winding roads into Devon resounded to the sound of motorcycles and cars. Football and cricket clubs resumed their seasonal schedules, and Devon's seaside resorts enjoyed another two decades of unrivalled prosperity – until victory had to be achieved once again.

About the Author

Formerly a headteacher in Hertfordshire and then a history lecturer, Masters Programme Director and European Masters Project Manager in the University of Plymouth's Faculty of Education, Dr David Parker has written several books and many articles for scholarly journals and popular magazines on nineteenth- and twentieth-century social history. He and his wife live in Exeter and they have two grown up children.

BIBLIOGRAPHY

Newspapers

Devon & Exeter Gazette
Exeter Express & Echo
Trewman's Exeter Flying Post
Western Evening Herald
Western Times

Devon Heritage Centre (County Archives and West Country Studies Library)

ECA/1/29-42   Exeter City Council minutes 1980–21
ECA/19/18-24   Exeter Education Committee minutes 1913–24
63/5/2/1-10   Maynard School Magazines 1914–18
68/3/1/7   Exeter, Rack Street Central School logbook
68/4/2/4   Exeter, St Thomas' Council School logbook
72/15/1/6   Exeter, Episcopal Girls' School logbook
75/15/1/2   Exeter, Episcopal Boys' School logbook
76/5/1/1   Exeter, Cowick Street Council School logbook
76/7/1/3   Exeter, Heavitree Church of England School logbook
76/16/2/2   Exeter, Newtown Council Boys' School logbook
1262M/O/O/LD/152/70   Earl Fortescue – war correspondence/reports
1262M/FH42   Earl Fortescue's memoirs
1262M/L112   Lord Lieutenancy 1914–19 files (including Red Cross files)
1262M/L141   Women and War Service files
1262M/L117 & L139   Exeter War Refugees Committee / Devon
    War Refugees Committee / Cornwall & Devon War Refugees
    Committee files
1262M/O/LD/141/1-60   Devon County Executive Food Committee files
1516M/add/F5/2   Nurse Braithwaite's common book and Hospital
    Magazine: Number 5 Temporary War Hospital

2065M/add/F325-344   Magazine of Number 1 Temporary War Hospital
2065M/add/F357   File of newspaper cuttings on Miss Georgiana Buller
2667M/FI   Ruth Whitaker's memoirs
4711Zadd/Z30   Messrs Willey's war work file
DCC 1/3/1 and 157/5/5/1   Maternity & Child Welfare Committee
    memoranda and correspondence 1913–19
DCC 5189M/Z1   Board of Education pamphlet: 'A Talk to School
    Children on Our Daily Bread'
Census of England & Wales for 1901 and 1911 – County of Devon, HMSO

Books & Articles

Aggett, W.J.P., *Bloody Eleventh: History of the Devons* (Devonshire &
    Dorset Regiment, 1995)
Andrews, L., *The Education Act, 1918* (Routledge & Kegan Paul, 1976)
Anon., 'In Memoriam, Dame Georgiana Buller 1883–1953' in *Journal
    of Bone & Joint Surgery, Volume 35B: Number 4* (1953)
Barlow, F., *Exeter and its Region* (University of Exeter Press, 1969)
Booker, F., *The Great Western Railway: A New History* (David &
    Charles, 2nd edition, 1985)
Constantine, S., Kirby, M.W., and Rose, M.B. (eds) T*he First World
    War in British History* (Edward Arnold, 1995)
DeGroot, G.J., *Blighty: British Society in the Era of the Great War*
    (Longman, 1996)
Fuller, F., *The History of St Luke's College, Exeter: Vol. 2 1886–1933*
    (Privately published, 1970)
Gilbert, M., *First World War* (Weidenfeld & Nicolson, 1988)
Harris, H., *Devon's Century of Change* (Peninsula Press, 1998)
Harris, J., *Private Lives, Public Spirit: Britain 1870–1914* (Penguin, 1993)
Hawkins, M., *LSWR West Country Lines: Then and Now*
    (Grange Books/Hawk Editions, 1999)
Holmes, R., *Tommy: The British Soldier on the Western Front*
    (Harper/Vintage, 2004)
Hoskins, W.G., *Two Thousand Years in Exeter* (James Townshend, 1960)
Hurt, J., *Elementary Schooling and the Working Classes 1860–1918*
    (Routledge & Kegan Paul, 1979)
Kelly's Directory of Devonshire 1914
Marwick, A*., The Deluge: British Society & the First World War*
    (The Bodley Head, 1965)
Newton, R., *Victorian Exeter 1837–1914* (Leicester University
    Press, 1968)
Orme, N. (Ed.), *Unity & Variety: A History of the Church in Devon and
    Cornwall* (University of Exeter Press, 1991
Parker, D., *The People of Devon in the First World War* (The History
    Press, 2013)
Pugh, M., *We Danced All Night: A Social History of Britain Between
    The Wars* (Vintage, 2009)
Russell, P.M.G., *A History of Exeter Hospitals 1170–1948*
    (James Townshend, 1976)

Simon, B., *Education & The Labour Movement 1870–1920*
(Lawrence & Wishart, 1965)
_____, *The Politics of Educational Reform, 1920–1940*
(Lawrence & Wishart, 1974)
Stevenson, D., *1914–1918: The History of the First World War*
(Penguin, 2004)
Stevenson, J., *British Society 1914–1945* (Pelican, 1984)
Travis, J.F., *The Rise of Devon Seaside Resorts 1750–1900*
(University of Exeter Press, 1993)
War diary of G. May, 1st Devon Battery, Royal Field Artillery
courtesy of Topsham Museum
Winter, J. and Baggett, B., *The Great War and the Shaping of the
Twentieth Century* (Penguin Studio, 1996)

Great War Britain:
The First World War at Home

Luci Gosling

After the declaration of war in 1914, the conflict dominated civilian life for the next four years. Magazines quickly adapted without losing their gossipy essence: fashion jostled for position with items on patriotic fundraising, and court presentations were replaced by notes on nursing. The result is a fascinating, amusing and uniquely feminine perspective of life on the home front.

978 0 7524 9188 2

The Workers' War:
British Industry and the First World War

Anthony Burton

The First World War didn't just rock the nation in terms of bloodshed: it was a war of technological and industrial advances. Working Britain experienced change as well: with the men at war, it fell to the women of the country to keep the factories going. Anthony Burton explores that change.

978 0 7524 9886 7

Visit our website and discover many other First World War books.

www.thehistorypress.co.uk/first-world-war